GLOBE

AMERICAN BIOGRAPHIES

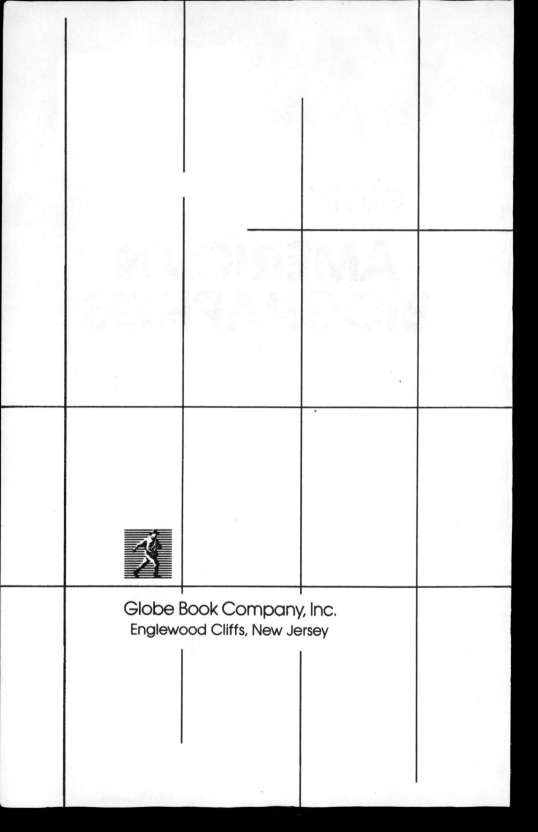

Globe Book Company, Inc.

Englewood Cliffs, New Jersey

GLOBE

AMERICAN BIOGRAPHIES

Henry I. Christ

Marie E. Christ
Contributing Author

Henry I. Christ has had a long, distinguished career as a writer, editor, and teacher. A specialist in language, literature, and composition, he is the author of several Globe books, including *Globe World Biographies, Modern Short Biographies, Short World Biographies, The World of Sports, The Challenge of Sports, The World of Careers,* and *Going Places.* In addition to his career as a writer, he is an active member of several professional organizations, and has served as Secretary of the Association of Chairmen in New York City Schools, Vice President of the New York State English Council, and Director of the National Council of Teachers of English. He has spoken at conventions and workshops throughout the United States, lectured on educational television, and frequently participates in curriculum development and evaluation. Henry I. Christ has written many articles for national educational periodicals, and was the editor of *High Points* for nearly 10 years. For the New York State Education Department, he has been a test consultant and a member of various committees on examinations.

Marie E. Christ has worked with Henry I. Christ throughout his career as teacher and writer. She played a major role in the development and preparation of this book.

Editor: Eileen Thompson
Illustrations: Robert Shore
Cover Design: Berg Design
Text Design: Mark Safran

ISBN: 0-87065-040-8

Printed in the United States of America   9   8   7   6   5   4   3

Contents

To the Student / vii

Unit 1   Breaking New Ground / 1
   Bill Cosby: *Comedian with a Serious Purpose* / 3
   Rosalyn Sussman Yalow: *Nobel Prize Winner* / 16
   •Bryant Gumbel: *Network News Star* / 28
   George Lucas and Steven Spielberg: *Masters of Fantasy* / 41
   Another Look / 56

Unit 2   Proving Leadership / 59
   Henry Cisneros: *Champion of the Cities* / 61
   Patricia Roberts Harris: *Member of the President's
      Cabinet* / 75
   Sequoyah: *Wizard of the Talking Leaves* / 88
   •Joe Montana: *"The Comeback Kid"* / 101
   Another Look / 116

Unit 3   Living for Adventure / 119
   Paul Newman: *Superstar* / 121
   Matthew Henson: *Arctic Explorer* / 136
   •Sacajawea: *Guide to the West* / 149
   Sally Ride: *First American Woman in Space* / 162
   Another Look / 176

Unit 4   Challenging Old Ideas / 179
    Susan L. Taylor: *Magazine Editor* / *181*
    Twyla Tharp: *Artist of the Dance* / *195*
    Lewis Thomas: *Scientist and Writer* / *208*
    Robert H. Goddard: *Rocket Pioneer* / *220*
    Another Look / *236*

Unit 5   Holding to the Course / 239
    Mary Lou Retton: *American Gymnast* / *241*
    Tom Selleck: *Television Star* / *253*
    Beverly Sills: *Famous Singer* / *266*
    Diana Ross: *Star of Pop Music* / *280*
    Another Look / *294*

To the Student

One of the most interesting topics in the world is *people*. You probably enjoy magazines that describe the lives of celebrities. You may watch television talk shows about people. In a variety of ways, you get a special pleasure in sharing other people's experiences. But do you ever wonder what makes some people act the way they do? In this book you will enjoy finding out about some special men and women.

Globe American Biographies is all about people. It enlarges your own experience through the experiences of others.

You will meet many different kinds of people in this book. Some are from the past, like the explorer Matthew Henson or the rocket pioneer Robert Goddard. Others are making headlines today, like Tom Selleck and Diana Ross. All are people worth knowing.

There is more to *Globe American Biographies* than people, though. Every person in the book is famous for contributing something to American life. Every achievement is important, from Henry Cisnero's program in San Antonio to Sally Ride's trips in the space shuttle. Every achievement will give you something to think about and to talk about.

The questions and other exercises in this book will help you to become a better reader. For example, the vocabulary exercises introduce important new words. Each word appears in a sentence that will help you learn its meaning.

Special sections called *Words at Your Service* show you how you can increase your vocabulary by watching for certain clues.

The quotations in the book are related to the subjects of the chapters and the units. Some are amusing; others are serious. All of them are interesting. In addition, each of them will serve as an interesting discussion starter.

When you have finished *Globe American Biographies* you will know more about people. You will also know more about America. Happy reading!

UNIT 1

BREAKING NEW GROUND

If a man does not keep pace with his companions, perhaps it is because he hears a different drummer. Let him step to the music that he hears, however measured or far away.

HENRY DAVID THOREAU

"That's a terrible idea. It won't work."

"I knew somebody who tried something like that. He failed."

"Why waste your time on that crazy new way of doing things? Why not do things the right way, the tested way?"

Comments like these have killed many good new ideas. But

now and then someone refuses
to listen. He or she just keeps
doing what seems right . . . and
succeeds.

This unit is devoted to people
with new ideas, people who
broke new ground. Around them
were many people who said,
"You'll fail." But the men and
women in this unit kept working along. They refused to admit
the possibility of failure. They
proved that new ideas can work.

Bill Cosby restored good taste
to the television situation comedy. Rosalyn Yalow proved that
women could succeed in a
"man's field." Bryant Gumbel
became the first black anchor on
a morning news show. Steven
Spielberg and George Lucas appealed to the imagination of
their audiences and reached for
the stars. After them came the
imitators.

BILL COSBY:
Comedian with a
Serious Purpose

*Take a lesson from the mosquito. He
never waits for an opening—he makes
one.*

KIRK KIRKPATRICK

By the autumn of 1984, television comedy was in trouble. The *New York Times* noted, "Sometime in the early 1980's, for reasons that are still being debated in Hollywood, the laughter dribbled out of television. The situation comedy . . . turned from a *vital* centerpiece in the medium to an endangered species, and nobody was exactly sure why."

Some blamed the shows of that time. In general, they said, the shows were without characters both interesting and believable. They depended too much on laugh tracks that made every little joke seem very funny. The *Times* said the laugh track had "destroyed *authentic* laughter on television for almost 10 years."

There were some bright spots, but the future of any new show seemed uncertain. Bill Cosby was not afraid to return excellence to the situation comedy. He decided to enter this field with a new show of his own. Not every network was interested.

"It's a bad time, Bill. You can't do that kind of show. You're taking too much of a chance."

Bill got a lot of *negative* advice, but he pressed on. Brandon Tartikoff of NBC liked Bill's plan. Bill's idea was to present a show with a new twist. It would have true-to-life characters in true-to-life situations. He decided to use an upper-middle-class black family. The father would be a successful doctor. The mother would be a successful lawyer. There would be five children. But the children would act like real children. The problems faced by the family would be real problems. They would not be the exaggerated triumphs and disasters of other situation comedies. They would be the kinds of problems mothers and fathers face all the time.

Black people had, of course, appeared in situation comedies before. Too often, though, they had been placed in exaggerated, false situations. Too often they had been stereotyped, put into false molds. In this show, blacks would be presented in a true way.

Some shows tried for easy laughs. Bill Cosby felt that laughs should come from a warm understanding of life's funny situations.

To keep the show on the right track, Bill brought in Dr. Alvin Poussaint. Dr. Poussaint has worked closely with Bill to make sure the people act in a real way. Dr. Poussaint has taken out of the show anything that is false or put in just for a laugh.

Because of Bill Cosby's reputation, many people watched his opening show. It was a big hit. Could it keep up its quality? Too often a series cannot hold to the high standards of the first one or two shows.

The second show was another big hit. People started to talk about it. "Have you seen *The Cosby Show?*" began to be heard every Friday in classrooms and offices across the United States. Bill had *defied* the odds and won. Week after week, the show kept up its high standards and held its audience. It gained a large share of the market and proved that good shows are always welcome.

A good show does not come about overnight. There were months of planning and hard work beforehand. It's not hard to put together a show that depends on one-line jokes. But audiences were getting tired of that kind of show, with its canned laughter. Bill wanted a show that brought out the interesting oddities of human nature. He wanted a show with characters that people could identify with.

The plot of a Bill Cosby show doesn't sound like much. One little daughter's pet goldfish dies. The parents tell the children to do their homework. The son comes home with an earring in his ear. The grandparents come for a visit. The son has his first shave. The son is asked to baby-sit. One daughter makes a shirt for her brother. One daughter has a boyfriend the parents do not like. Situations like these happen in many homes. What makes this show so special?

Families like the parents' warmth and understanding. They see that the parents' ability to find humor in little difficulties shows true maturity. The love between the parents shines in every show. The children in the television family feel secure in that love. They are normal children, sometimes causing trouble. But in all the shows the warm good humor flows.

From idea to show is not an easy, straight line. Bill wants everything perfect. His standards are high. He expects a lot from his writers. The first group had agreed to write six shows. At the end of that period, three of the four left the show. As one writer said, "Bill challenges you to do your best, but I must say that I was awfully tired."

Bill hired six new writers. They included the show's first two black writers. Bill sees no color differences. Human problems are the same for all people.

Cosby is hard on his writers, but he's also hard on his cast. In forming his TV family, Bill imitated his own family. In real life, he has four daughters and a son. On the show he has four daughters and a son. The active family on the show does not include the oldest daughter, who is away at college. As in real life, Bill is a strict but loving father figure.

Bill chose his cast carefully, and the parts are well played. He wants his child actors to play their roles professionally, but they don't object. Tempestt Bledsoe, who plays the next-to-the-youngest daughter, was once scolded for missing a line. She was not upset. She realized he was right. Later she said, "He has a secret theory about kids. He can walk up to kids and start playing with them. And he can make kids behave without telling them to do so."

The TV children play normal children, the same in life

as on the show. Although the children are mostly new to television, they are born professionals. They respect Bill. That is no surprise. His real-life children are taught respect for others. They respect Bill, other adults, and each other. It was easy for Bill to create his role on this show. He played himself.

Bill's real-life family gets along well with his television family. The real-life children enjoy the show children. The two wives enjoy each other's company. Phylicia Rashad says she has learned a lot from playing Bill's show wife. "I'm a better parent since the series."

Bill likes to turn things upside down. He attacks the usual worn-out sentiments of poor shows. In one show the son defended his poor grades. He said he didn't want to be a success. He just wanted to be a regular person, to be himself. At this point the audience clapped loudly. This is the kind of reaction expected of them in most shows. Bill waited a moment and said, "That's about the dumbest thing I've ever heard." The audience gasped, laughed, and clapped. Bill refuses to accept the dull and commonplace.

The Cosby Show is taped before a live audience. This plan puts an extra burden on the actors, but it also adds something. The actors can play to the audience. They can see how their lines are going over. They can feel the audience's good will. There are technical problems and cast errors, though. It usually takes more than two hours to complete the half-hour show. But the audience enjoys seeing how a show is put together. They also enjoy seeing a master performer at work under trying circumstances.

Praise for *The Cosby Show* was not long in coming. His program won the "February Sweeps." This means that it was the most popular show of the month. Then on March 14, 1985, the People's Choice Awards honored Bill Cosby and his program. He was voted the favorite male performer in a new TV series. His program won as top TV comedy and favorite new show. His co-star, Phylicia Rashad, was selected as favorite female performer in a new TV series.

The success of *The Cosby Show* was no accident. Bill Cosby didn't suddenly stumble onto a good idea. He didn't come out of nowhere to become successful overnight. He has worked long and hard. But his career has been solid and rewarding.

Bill was born in Philadelphia in 1937. He used his early life in that city for comic ideas later on. In the fifth grade he did his first comedy routine. It was well liked by his teacher and classmates. After leaving school, he joined the Navy and served four years. In 1961 he went to Temple University on an athletic scholarship. He played right halfback on the football team. Professional scouts wanted him for their teams. He chose another field.

He became a comic. He could tell stories well, and this won him a wide following. In 1965 television producer Sheldon Leonard saw him in one of Cosby's shows. He gave Cosby a screen test, and Cosby became nationally known. That year he joined Robert Culp in a television series, *I Spy*. Bill received two Emmy awards for his acting in that show. He was the first black to co-star in a weekly television show.

Bill is a born teacher. Those who work with him learn from him. In 1977 he received a special degree from the University of Massachusetts. He welcomes challenges. By 1984 Bill was ready for a new challenge. *The Cosby Show* was the answer.

Bill Cosby's talents were noticed early on. In 1965 the writer Charles L. Mee, Jr., wrote, "There *lurks,* just over Cosby's shoulder, something more than just a comedian, and one day that quality may fully *emerge.*"

That day has arrived.

UNDERSTANDING WHAT YOU HAVE READ

Finding Another Title

1. Another good title for this selection might be (a) Bill Cosby and Television Comedy (b) The Rise and Fall of a Television Star (c) Bill Cosby: Man of Many Moods (d) How to Make a Television Show.

Getting the Main Idea

2. The most important reason for Bill Cosby's success is that he (a) was lucky in the people he chose for his show (b) knew Brandon Tartikoff (c) brought real human values to the show (d) had played a different kind of role on another show.

Finding Details

3. Bill Cosby's TV family (a) uses three actors from Bill's real family (b) has two sons and three daughters (c) has the same number of children as Bill's real family (d) has one daughter and four sons.
4. Tempestt Bledsoe is (a) a television critic (b) a member of the Cosby cast (c) a television writer (d) the person who discovered Bill Cosby.
5. One sport in which Bill Cosby was skilled is (a) baseball (b) soccer (c) tennis (d) football.
6. Sheldon Leonard is mentioned as a (a) writer (b) actor (c) director (d) producer.
7. Bill Cosby was put into his first television series in (a) 1961 (b) 1965 (c) 1977 (d) 1984.

8. Robert Culp is a (a) producer (b) writer on *The Cosby Show* (c) winner of two Emmy awards (d) fellow actor.

9. *I Spy* is the name of (a) a television series (b) a single episode of *The Cosby Show* (c) the talk Bill Cosby gave at a graduation ceremony (d) a biography of Bill Cosby.

10. The University of Massachusetts (a) awarded Bill Cosby a special degree (b) gave Cosby an athletic scholarship (c) is Dr. Poussaint's school (d) provided sets for *The Cosby Show*.

Making Inferences

11. The *New York Times* thinks the television laugh track is (a) useful for getting people in the mood (b) a rarely used way of making a show more cheerful (c) a bad influence on television comedy (d) a harmless tool, even if a bit dishonest.

12. Brandon Tartikoff (a) hesitated about accepting Bill's idea (b) had a great deal of faith in Bill (c) did not like Bill's type of comedy (d) insisted on taking creative control of the show.

13. *The Cosby Show* did well because it (a) had a lot of clever one-line jokes (b) truly revealed the black experience (c) presented people that everyone could identify with (d) showed two professional people in a silly situation.

14. Bill most likely thinks Alvin Poussaint is (a) important for the success of the show (b) a bother (c) an excellent writer of comedy (d) a good choice for a member of the cast.

15. When *The Cosby Show* began, it was aired on (a) Fridays (b) Thursdays (c) Saturdays (d) Mondays.

Predicting What Happens Next

16. After the first six shows, the new writers most likely **(a)** completely changed the show **(b)** made the mother much more likable than the father **(c)** disagreed with Bill on the show's direction **(d)** tried to build on the success of the first shows.

Deciding on the Order of Events

17. The following events are scrambled. Arrange them in proper order, as they happened. Use letters only.
(a) Bill joins the Navy.
(b) Sheldon Leonard sees Bill in a show.
(c) Bill attends Temple University.
(d) Bill performs his first comedy routine.

Inferring Tone

18. The attitude of the *New York Times* (4) toward the typical television comedy show of the early 1980s is one of **(a)** respect **(b)** scorn **(c)** deep hatred **(d)** amusement.

Separating Facts from Opinions

For each of the following, tell whether the statement is a fact (*F*) or an opinion (*O*).
19. Bill Cosby co-starred in a television series in 1965.
20. The 1965 television series was the best show of its kind at that time.

Understanding Words from Context

21. The situation comedy turned from a *vital* centerpiece to an unimportant and endangered species.

Vital (4) means (a) humorous (b) frequently watched (c) important (d) cheerful.

22. Since it contained fake laughter, the laugh track had destroyed *authentic* laughter on television for almost 10 years.

Authentic (4) means (a) hearty (b) true (c) canned (d) forced.

23. Bill had *defied* the odds and won.

Defied (5) means (a) studied (b) yielded to (c) discovered (d) challenged.

24. Charles L. Mee, Jr., wrote, "There *lurks*, just over Cosby's shoulder, something more than just a comedian. . . ."

Lurks (8) means (a) waits out of sight (b) shines brightly (c) disappears (d) dances noisily.

25. Although that quality is not easy to see now, one day it may fully *emerge*.

Emerge (8) means (a) sink out of sight (b) disappear for a brief time (c) come into view (d) develop quietly.

THINKING IT OVER

1. Have you ever seen *The Cosby Show?* Do you consider it a good show? Explain your answer.
2. Bill Cosby says that basically all people have the same problems. How did Cosby demonstrate that belief?
3. Do you feel that the laugh track helps television comedy? Why or why not?
4. How did Bill Cosby show his devotion to the ideal of quality in television?
5. What part do luck and good timing play in success? Can a person succeed even if the timing is wrong? Explain.

6. What are some of the problems involved in putting on a weekly television series?
7. Look up the word *syndication* in your dictionary. What is *syndication?* Some actors make more money from *syndication* than from original performances. Can you explain why?
8. Everyday events are filled with humor if we look closely enough. Can you give an example from your own life?

ANOTHER LOOK AT THE QUOTATION

> *Take a lesson from the mosquito. He never waits for an opening—he makes one.*
>
> KIRK KIRKPATRICK

1. Explain the quotation in your own words.
2. How did Bill Cosby demonstrate the truth of this quotation?
3. What is the tone, or attitude, of this quotation: serious, humorous, or angry?
4. How did Bill Cosby show intelligence throughout his life?

WORDS AT YOUR SERVICE—WHAT IS CONTEXT?

"It's a bad time, Bill. You can't do that kind of show. You're taking too much of a chance."
Bill got a lot of *negative* advice. (4)

Even if you had never seen the word *negative* before, you'd have a good idea of its meaning. You'd notice all those comments telling Bill not to do a show. You'd realize that negative advice says, "Don't do it!" All those words around *negative* are called its *context. Context* may be a new and unfamiliar word to you, but it is a very important word. Understanding context is the key to hundreds of new words.

Context may involve real situations as well as words. Suppose someone says to you, "Please hand me that awl" and points to a tool. You'll immediately know what an *awl* is. The total context gives you a new word. You have learned most of the words in your vocabulary by this kind of context.

You have also learned a great many words by context in reading and listening. Someone may say, "When I'm tired, I become *irritable.*" Even if *irritable* is a new word for you, as you read it, you know what happens when *you* become tired. You make a good guess at the meaning of *irritable: touchy, grouchy, cranky.*

Context can help you learn many new words. The next eight chapters will give you all kinds of clues to help you enlarge your vocabulary and master many new words.

Study the following sentences and then guess at the meaning of each *italicized* word. Use the entire sentence to help you.

EXAMPLE

Just as I was thinking of my sister Ruth, the phone rang, and Ruth's voice called, "How are you?" What a *coincidence* this was!
Coincidence means **(a)** pleasant surprise **(b)** shock **(c)** things happening at the same time **(d)** special kind of communication.

The sentence talks about two events occurring at the same time: thinking of Ruth and getting the call from Ruth. The correct answer is **(c)** *things happening at the same time.*

1. There was such an *abundance* of food that no one went hungry.
   Abundance means **(a)** plenty **(b)** shortage **(c)** sameness **(d)** complete lack.
2. When Jeremy spoke in his usual slow style, his classmates cruelly began to *mock* him.
   Mock means **(a)** praise **(b)** make fun of **(c)** be proud of **(d)** encourage.
3. Juan is agreeable when he gets his way, but *mulish* when he doesn't.
   Mulish means **(a)** likable **(b)** talented **(c)** happy **(d)** stubborn.
4. That tea is too strong for me. Please *dilute* it with hot water.
   Dilute means **(a)** make larger **(b)** weaken by mixing **(c)** sweeten, as with sugar **(d)** make more enjoyable.
5. Facing a job interview was a frightening ordeal for Rita, but she walked into the interview room and didn't *flinch*.
   Flinch means **(a)** laugh **(b)** skip **(c)** win out **(d)** draw back.

ROSALYN SUSSMAN YALOW:

Nobel Prize Winner

When somebody is happy, he does not hear the clock strike.

GERMAN PROVERB

Have you ever stayed up late watching the Academy Awards show? If you have, you have sensed the importance of these prizes. Careers are often made by people being named for a prize and by their winning one. The Oscar, the symbol of *recognition,* stands proudly in the home of many a star.

The Academy Award is one of many prizes. In fact, there seem to be prizes in every field. There are Grammy Awards in recording and Emmy Awards in television. There are Tony Awards in the theater and Peabody Awards in broadcasting. There are Sullivan Awards in athletics and Pulitzer Prizes in literature. The list goes on and on. There is, however, one prize that stands head and shoulders above all the rest: the Nobel Prize.

The Nobel Prizes were first given in 1901 with money from the will of Alfred Nobel. The Nobel Peace Prize is given in Oslo, Norway. The name suggests its purpose: to honor an outstanding man or woman of peace. Prizes in other areas are given each year in Stockholm, Sweden. With these prizes, the Swedish Royal Academy of Science seeks to honor outstanding achievement in chemistry, physics, medicine, literature, and economics.

The list of Nobel Prize winners is an honor roll of our times. Many American writers have won the Nobel Prize in Literature. Sinclair Lewis, Eugene O'Neill, Pearl S. Buck, Ernest Hemingway, and John Steinbeck have been among those honored. Prize winners in medicine are less well known, but their achievements deserve the world's thanks. For example, Frederick Banting of Canada was a co-winner of the prize in medicine in 1923. He shared the prize with John Macleod of Scotland for their discovery of insulin. In 1977 an American scientist became the second woman ever to win the Nobel Prize in Medicine. Rosalyn Sussman Yalow richly deserved one of the world's highest honors.

Rosalyn Sussman Yalow was born on July 19, 1921, in the Bronx, New York. She was not born into wealth. But her parents believed in education. Her father, Simon Sussman, often said, "Girls can do anything boys can do." When Rosalyn was growing up, there were few women in some of the higher science fields. But Rosalyn believed she could do well in these fields.

A chemistry teacher at Walton High School saw in Rosalyn the qualities of a good scientist and urged her to major in science. She developed this interest further. When Rosalyn entered Hunter College, in New York City, she majored in physics.

Graduate training costs a lot of money. College advisers suggested that Rosalyn take courses in shorthand and typing. This way she could get an office job. Then she could support herself in graduate school. Rosalyn took the advice, but she did not need her office skills. She graduated from Hunter College with honors in physics and chemistry and was offered a teaching job at the University of Illinois.

She taught in the College of Engineering. There were 400 men on the faculty—and one woman: Rosalyn Sussman. One man in particular was very much taken with Rosalyn. A. Aaron Yalow and Rosalyn were married in 1943. Two years later they both earned their Ph.D. degrees from Illinois. Dr. Rosalyn Yalow became the second woman in history to get the degree in physics from that university.

The two scientists had a good life together. Their marriage was an ideal mix. They were partners but also individuals. They helped and supported each other. But they developed their own talents and treated each other as equals.

Rosalyn Yalow seemed to live many lives all at once. The years between graduating and receiving the Nobel

Prize were filled with great activity. She did important research. She published more than three hundred articles. An outstanding speaker, she gave many *distinguished* talks. She was awarded several honorary degrees. She became an important member of many scientific societies.

Dr. Yalow joined the staff of the Veterans Administration hospital in the Bronx. She served on national committees. She was a member of the president's Study Group on Careers for Women. She worked on a professional journal. In 1978 she was the host for a TV show on the life of Marie Curie. In addition to this work, she raised two children, kept a garden, cooked, kept house, and maintained a happy home life.

Winning the Nobel Prize demands something truly special. What did Dr. Yalow do? With Dr. Solomon A. Berson she began to study thyroid disease. Their studies led them to look at the make-up of blood. They started out to measure certain elements in the blood. But methods available then were just not suitable.

They used radioactive iodine in their tests. They came up with new ways of analyzing blood. They studied how the body makes and destroys certain substances. Unlike older, inexact ways, their new methods gave a *precise* way to measure the concentration of certain substances in the blood.

What they found was useful in unexpected ways. In their work with diabetes, they found some common mistakes. They went further. They found a way to tell whether a person with an ulcer needs an operation. They measured the amount of growth hormone in the bodies of certain undersized children. In this way, they could tell whether these children could be helped. They studied tumors and kidney stones.

Today their method is used in nearly all medical fields. It is now used to screen blood in blood banks. It is helpful in work with drug addiction. Doctors are grateful for the new tool supplied by Dr. Yalow and Dr. Berson.

Dr. Yalow rose in her field. She first became acting chief of an important division of the Veterans Administration hospital and then chief. Then she became director of the Solomon A. Berson Research Laboratory. During the busy 1950s, her advice was often sought. For example, she served as *consultant* at Lenox Hill Hospital in Manhattan. She became research professor at the Mount Sinai School of Medicine.

A year before receiving the Nobel Prize, she became the first woman ever to win the Albert Lasker Prize for Basic Medical Research. Then she was given $72,500 in prize money for the Nobel Prize. She banked the money and said, "I can't think of anything I want. I wasn't handed college or graduate school or anything else on a silver platter. I had to work very hard, but I did it because I wanted to. That's the real key to happiness."

Dr. Yalow remembers her father's encouraging words about the possibilities open to women. When she was given her prize at the Nobel Festival in Stockholm, she said, "If women are to start moving toward that goal of equality with men, we must believe in ourselves." Then she went on, "We must feel a personal responsibility to ease the path for those who come after us. The world cannot afford the loss of the talents of half its people if we are to solve the many problems that *beset* us."

Her own life provides a model to admire. She often puts in an eighty-hour week, but she is rarely tired. She told an interviewer, "I can't think of anything in the world that I would want that I haven't had. I have my marriage, two wonderful children. I have a laboratory that is an absolute joy. I have energy. I have health. As long as there is anything to be done, I am never tired."

Can't is a word not in Dr. Yalow's vocabulary.

UNDERSTANDING WHAT YOU HAVE READ

Finding Another Title

1. Another good title for this selection might be (a) The Joys of Science (b) How the Nobel Prizes Are Awarded (c) How to Find Happiness (d) Woman Pioneer in Medicine.

Getting the Main Idea

2. Rosalyn Sussman Yalow (a) has lived a rich and well-balanced life (b) married a fellow science student (c) used radioactive iodine in an experiment (d) showed promise while in high school.

Finding Details

3. Peabody Awards are given in (a) athletics (b) literature (c) broadcasting (d) recording.
4. All the following won a Nobel Prize in Literature EXCEPT (a) Pearl S. Buck (b) A. Aaron Yalow (c) John Steinbeck (d) Sinclair Lewis.
5. Dr. Yalow was first persuaded to major in science by (a) a college professor (b) a high school chemistry teacher (c) her father (d) Dr. Solomon Berson.
6. Rosalyn took courses in shorthand and typing to (a) begin work as secretary to the president (b) support herself through graduate school (c) satisfy her curiosity about language (d) write letters to business firms to ask for jobs.
7. When Dr. Yalow received her degree in physics from the University of Illinois, she was (a) the first woman to do so (b) the second woman to do so (c) denied a job there (d) not yet married.

8. During her important work in medicine, Dr. Yalow worked closely with **(a)** Solomon A. Berson **(b)** Marie Curie **(c)** Albert Lasker **(d)** her husband.
9. Dr. Yalow and her fellow worker began their study on **(a)** ulcers **(b)** growth in children **(c)** thyroid disease **(d)** drug addiction.
10. All the following are mentioned as Dr. Yalow's activities EXCEPT **(a)** acting in a Broadway play **(b)** serving on the staff of the Veterans Administration hospital **(c)** publishing more than 300 articles **(d)** being awarded several honorary degrees.

Making Inferences

11. Dr. Yalow received her Nobel Prize in **(a)** Illinois **(b)** Oslo **(c)** the Bronx **(d)** Stockholm.
12. Simon Sussman **(a)** urged Rosalyn to go to work after high school **(b)** was a great scientist **(c)** greatly influenced his daughter's life **(d)** had an old-fashioned idea about the role of women.
13. The marriage of Aaron and Rosalyn Yalow worked well because **(a)** they shared every experience **(b)** they respected each other as individuals **(c)** they had children **(d)** they spent vacations together.
14. This selection shows that important discoveries often **(a)** have unexpected uses **(b)** bring misery to their discoverers **(c)** are forgotten within months **(d)** make enemies of former friends.
15. Dr. Yalow believes firmly in **(a)** luck **(b)** the superiority of women **(c)** taking wild chances **(d)** hard work.

Predicting What Happens Next

16. After receiving the Nobel Prize, Dr. Yalow most likely **(a)** took a year off to rest **(b)** changed the course of her life **(c)** went back to work **(d)** took a refresher course in secretarial work.

Deciding on the Order of Events

17. The following events are scrambled. Arrange them in proper order, as they happened. Use letters only.
(a) She is host for a series on Marie Curie.
(b) She marries A. Aaron Yalow.
(c) She wins the Nobel Prize.
(d) She enrolls in the College of Engineering at the University of Illinois.

Inferring Tone

18. The tone of Dr. Yalow's Stockholm address is **(a)** bitter **(b)** comforting **(c)** inspiring **(d)** boastful.

Separating Facts from Opinions

For each of the following, tell whether the statement is a fact (*F*) or an opinion (*O*).
19. Eugene O'Neill won a Nobel Prize in Literature.
20. More women should be awarded Nobel Prizes.

Understanding Words from Context

21. The Oscar, the symbol of *recognition,* stands proudly in the home of many a star.
Recognition (17) means **(a)** hard work **(b)** good

fortune (c) disappointment (d) special attention.

22. An outstanding speaker, she delivered many *distinguished* talks.
    Distinguished (19) means (a) little noticed (b) fault finding (c) well attended (d) excellent.
23. Unlike older, inexact ways, their new methods gave a *precise* way to measure the concentration of certain substances in the blood.
    Precise (19) means (a) novel (b) exact (c) colorful (d) rough.
24. During the busy 1950s, her advice was often sought. For example, she served as *consultant* at Lenox Hill Hospital in Manhattan.
    Consultant (20) means (a) surgeon (b) reporter (c) adviser (d) legal aide.
25. The world cannot afford the loss of the talents of half its people if we are to solve the many problems that *beset* us.
    Beset (20) means (a) trouble (b) amuse (c) please (d) control.

THINKING IT OVER

1. How did Rosalyn Sussman Yalow prove that a woman can succeed in what was once considered a man's field?
2. Have you ever watched any of the awards programs, like the Academy Awards? What do you like about them? What do you dislike about them?
3. Some people think there are too many awards shows on television. Do you agree? Explain.
4. What special abilities does Dr. Yalow possess?

5. How important was Dr. Yalow's father to her career? Suppose a young person plans to become a plumber even though his or her parents would prefer another occupation. What should the young person do?
6. Medicine is making progress every day. We often hear of new advances in medicine. Can you describe one?

ANOTHER LOOK AT THE QUOTATION

When someone is happy, he does not hear the clock strike.

GERMAN PROVERB

1. Explain the quotation in your own words.
2. How did Dr. Yalow show she was happy? Did she ever hear the clock strike?
3. "Work at what you enjoy. Enjoy whatever you work at." This is good advice. Is it always possible to enjoy your work? Explain.
4. "If you can't have what you want, want what you have." This saying is like question 3 above. Is it possible to learn to be satisfied with what you have? Explain.
5. A proverb usually contains a lot of wisdom. Yet proverbs can conflict:

    Look before you leap.
    He who hesitates is lost.

How can you explain the difference in the advice given? (Remember that proverbs talk about wisdom generally, but sometimes individual cases go against general advice.)

WORDS AT YOUR SERVICE—THE SENTENCE AS A WHOLE

The world cannot afford the loss of the talents of half its people if we are to solve the many problems that *beset* us. (20)

The word *beset* was probably new to you. But notice how its surroundings help. In the last chapter you learned that a word's context is its surrounding words. Here, all of the sentence gives you a clue to the meaning of *beset*. The sentence speaks up for the contribution of women to society (half its people). Then it mentions the need to solve the problems that *beset* us. Problems must be solved. Problems trouble us. We can make a good guess that *beset* means something like *trouble*.

Study the following sentences and then guess the meaning of each *italicized* word. Let the entire sentence help you.

EXAMPLE

My little sister is too *contrary* to follow any suggestions.
Contrary means (a) friendly (b) happy (c) unwilling and self-willed (d) powerful.
If the little sister won't follow suggestions, she must be (c) unwilling and self-willed.

1. When I was asked a question, I was suddenly embarrassed because I had a *momentary* loss of memory.
    Momentary means (a) frightening (b) temporary (c) thoughtful (d) expected.
2. By cutting off trade, a *boycott* might hurt a company's business chances.

Boycott means **(a)** refusal to buy **(b)** advertising **(c)** a sales campaign **(d)** change of management.

3. At the *adjournment* of the meeting, all members left the auditorium.

   Adjournment means **(a)** report **(b)** beginning **(c)** announcement **(d)** conclusion.

4. For farmers to *prosper,* they need good weather and good growing conditions.

   Prosper means **(a)** get a loan **(b)** lose money **(c)** succeed **(d)** win a race.

5. From a diameter of an inch, the pipe *tapered* down to a quarter of an inch.

   Tapered means **(a)** played **(b)** narrowed **(c)** grew **(d)** reflected.

BRYANT GUMBEL:
Network News Star

Consider the postage stamp, my son. Its usefulness consists in its ability to stick to one thing until it gets there.

JOSH BILLINGS

Television news is a battlefield. News shows are well liked. Advertisers are willing to pay a lot of money to get their messages across to listeners. These listeners become attached to certain shows, certain newscasters. They often stay with their favorites. Well-liked newscasters are valuable. If they bring in the listeners and hold them, television stations and the networks are ready to pay them huge salaries.

There are two major kinds of news shows: local and national. National shows are seen on many stations within a network. Local shows are seen in a smaller area. They report local happenings, like accidents, home-team sports, doings of local people. They often have four regulars: a man and a woman to report the news, a weather person, and a sports reporter.

National network programs are a little different. Evening shows usually feature one person, called the *anchor*. Anchors are usually known across the country—for example, Peter Jennings at ABC, Tom Brokaw at NBC, and Dan Rather at CBS. They have assistant newscasters who handle special items like business news, sports, and entertainment.

The morning network shows often have co-anchors, a man and a woman. Together they are responsible for the news. The networks fight hard for listeners. They try to get the best people for these important jobs.

For years the NBC morning *Today* show featured Tom Brokaw and Jane Pauley. In 1981 Brokaw left the morning show to anchor the evening news. His departure left a gap that was hard to fill. NBC began looking for someone to take his place. The *Today* show had been losing listeners for several years. Finding the right person was very important. Then someone said, "Let's get Bryant Gumbel!"

In January 1982 Bryant Gumbel joined the *Today* show.

At first, NBC tried a three-person team, with Gumbel, Jane Pauley, and Chris Wallace. Then NBC took a gamble and dropped the three-person idea. The new plan gave Gumbel a major role. He worked well with Jane Pauley and *justified* NBC's confidence.

Gumbel had won about 72 million viewers in his work reporting sports. Many of them liked him and began to turn to see him on *Today.* Gradually the show gained a wider audience. It far outdistanced CBS and began to catch up with favored ABC. Gumbel became a welcome visitor in many American homes every morning.

What route did Gumbel take to gain so important a job? He was by no means an overnight sensation. He had worked hard. He began his career as a writer. He wrote a number of articles for *Black Sports,* a national sports magazine. Then at twenty-two he became its editor. A television executive invited Bryant to *audition* for a job. He accepted and became a weekend sportscaster for KNBC-TV in Los Angeles. A year later he became a daily sportscaster.

By 1975 Bryant had become known across the country. He was a co-host of the NBC Sports' National Football League pre-game show. In December 1976, he became the sports director of KNBC. He kept that job until July 1980. At the same time, he was handling other jobs. He covered basketball and baseball as well as football. A year after he became sports director, the network itself, NBC, asked him to co-host *Grandstand.* This show offered live events, features, and sports news. For five years Bryant held down two jobs, one in New York and one in Los Angeles.

In September 1980 Bryant started to appear on the *Today* show. Three times a week, he gave sports reports that won critical praise. When Tom Brokaw moved to the evening news show, Bryant Gumbel was ready to take over his job.

As the first black anchor of a network morning program, Bryant Gumbel has broken new ground. He has provided a good role model. He has been called "the most influential black newscaster in America."

What is the source of Bryant's popularity? He describes himself as "not so handsome as to be threatening, nor so appealing as to cause viewers to turn off their TV sets." The experts say that people reporting the news must first be accepted and then believed. Bryant has proved over and over again that he can do this.

As a newscaster and interviewer for *Today*, Bryant is in the big leagues. He meets some of the most important people in the world. In September 1984, *Today* showed Bryant Gumbel's interviews with several important leaders of the Soviet Union. Bryant's was a difficult and dangerous task. James H. Billington, an expert on Russia, said, "Gumbel was simply the best I have ever seen at posing hard questions to the Russians."

For his work in Moscow, the Overseas Press Club gave Bryant the Edward R. Murrow prize for outstanding foreign affairs work. For his Moscow reporting, Georgetown University honored him with its Edward Weintal prize.

Bryant travels a great deal. In 1985 *Today* was televised from Vietnam. During Easter Week of that year, Bryant and the *Today* show went to Rome for an audience with Pope John Paul II. If you telephone Bryant's office, you may be told he's out west, down south, or out of the country.

By the time Bryant talked with those Soviet leaders in Moscow, he had come a long way from his beginnings. He was born on September 29, 1948, in New Orleans and was raised in Chicago. His father was a judge in Chicago. Bryant earned a liberal arts degree from Bates College in Maine in 1970.

Bryant's father always stressed the importance of communication. Both Bryant and his brother Greg were impressed by this home training. Like Bryant, Greg is in television as a sportscaster.

Bryant is very much aware of how much he owes to his father. He has a framed picture of him in his office. He will point to the picture and say, "Whatever I am in this business, whatever I am in life, and whatever I've learned, I owe it to him."

Bryant has a lively personality. In many ways he is an *extravert*—that is, he usually doesn't keep things locked inside himself. He says, "People who know me never have to look for me. When I'm mad, they know it; when I'm happy, they know it. I do very few things in *moderation*."

Bryant says that nothing frightens him in his job. He says there are several reasons. "Number one is, I'm a cocky son of a gun and always have been: and constantly believe that I'll always wind up on my feet. The second reason why I'm not afraid is that I've never considered this (job) any big deal."

Job pressures often hurt family life. Bryant has kept them away from his family. On his wall are more than 30 pictures of his wife, June, his son, Bradley Christopher, and his daughter, Jillian Beth. Bryant likes his privacy when he's not on the air. He says, "I love my family— away from here I fall somewhere between a hermit and a *recluse*. Like most people who become parents, I learn a great deal on a daily basis, things that . . . seem petty when you talk about them in public."

Bryant puts everything into place. He says, "My family is important to me, my work is important to me, my self-respect and good name are important to me. The other things take care of themselves."

Many young people would like to get into television and become stars. The road is difficult. For these people, Bryant has some good advice.

"The first thing they should do is to be terribly sure that that's what they want to do. Because it's *frustrating,* and there's no way of measuring whether or not you're getting to where you want to be. I'm fortunate. If I had had any frustrations, I probably wouldn't be sitting here."

Bryant has made his mark through hard work and natural ability. Steve Friedman, the producer of *Today,* says, "He's born to be in television. No one does television better."

UNDERSTANDING WHAT YOU HAVE READ

Finding Another Title

1. Another good title for this selection might be **(a)** Understanding the News **(b)** Evening Network Shows on Television **(c)** A Black Role Model on Network Television **(d)** How Television Chooses Network News Shows.

Getting the Main Idea

2. Which of the following best states the main idea of the selection?
   (a) The networks think that certain programs are important for making money.
   (b) Bryant Gumbel has been outstanding in all the jobs he has had.
   (c) Newspapers are more interesting than network news.
   (d) Sports reporting on the air is more challenging than news reporting.

Finding Details

3. All of these people are named as regular members of local television news teams EXCEPT (a) business reporter (b) man newscaster (c) woman newscaster (d) weather person.
4. The most important reporter on a television news show is called the (a) pilot (b) anchor (c) leader (d) captain.
5. All the following are correctly matched EX- CEPT (a) Peter Jennings—ABC (b) Bryant Gumbel—NBC (c) Dan Rather—CBS (d) Jane Pauley—ABC.
6. The person who was dropped from the *Today* three- person team is (a) Chris Wallace (b) Edward R. Murrow (c) Steve Friedman (d) Greg Gumbel.
7. Bryant Gumbel used to do the pre-game show for (a) volley ball (b) football (c) basketball (d) hockey.
8. Bryant was given a prize for his talks with leaders of (a) France (b) Great Britain (c) China (d) the Soviet Union.
9. Bryant was born in (a) New Orleans (b) New York (c) Chicago (d) Los Angeles.
10. The person who has influenced Bryant the most was his (a) sister (b) brother (c) father (d) mother.

Making Inferences

11. Many shows have a man and a woman as co-anchors because (a) Brokaw started the idea (b) this plan provides a better balance (c) women are better at talking to people than men are (d) this plan gives jobs to more people.

12. Tom Brokaw most likely went to the evening news show **(a)** because he didn't get along with his co-host **(b)** to move closer to home **(c)** because the network thought the change would help ratings **(d)** to help his closest friend, Bryant Gumbel.

13. It is reasonable to say that Bryant Gumbel **(a)** is lucky, but not especially skilled **(b)** had Tom Brokaw moved **(c)** is more popular with men than with women **(d)** has a large following.

14. The *Today* show sent Bryant to many places around the world **(a)** because Bryant likes to travel **(b)** to keep the show interesting **(c)** to save money **(d)** so that foreigners can see Bryant Gumbel in person.

15. Bryant Gumbel's career suggests that he is **(a)** lively **(b)** without a sense of humor **(c)** never upset **(d)** unhappy.

Predicting What Happens Next

16. After Bryant Gumbel's trip to Vietnam, NBC probably **(a)** allowed him to travel, but only once each year **(b)** replaced Gumbel with another interviewer **(c)** let Bryant interview only in New York **(d)** continued to send him to newsworthy spots.

Deciding on the Order of Events

17. The following events are scrambled. Arrange them in proper order, as they happened. Use letters only.
(a) Bryant talks with the Russian leaders.
(b) Tom Brokaw leaves the *Today* show.
(c) Bryant attends Bates College.
(d) NBC chooses Bryant for the *Today* show.

Inferring Tone

18. When Steve Friedman talked about Bryant and television (33), he spoke in (a) anger (b) disappointment (c) mild approval (d) admiration.

Separating Facts from Opinions

For each of the following, tell whether the statement is a fact (*F*) or an opinion (*O*).
19. On a news show a weather person is more important than a sportscaster.
20. Jane Pauley was co-anchor of the *Today* show with Bryant Gumbel.

Understanding Words from Context

21. Bryant showed the network executives that they were right in giving him such an important job. He worked well with Jane Pauley and *justified* NBC's confidence.
    Justified (30) means (a) provided good reason for (b) failed (c) won (d) gave away.
22. A television executive wanted to see if Bryant would do well. He invited him to *audition* for a job.
    Audition (30) means (a) telephone (b) write an article (c) try out (d) relax.
23. "When I'm mad, they know it; when I'm happy, they know it. I do very few things in *moderation*."
    Moderation (32) means (a) without overdoing (b) anger (c) joy (d) a loud voice.
24. Bryant likes his privacy when he's not on television. He says, "I love my family—away from here I fall somewhere between a hermit and a *recluse*."

A *recluse* (32) **(a)** rarely sees other people **(b)** finds fault with close friends **(c)** enjoys showing off in public **(d)** enjoys new and different experiences.

25. He says about television work, "It's *frustrating,* and there's no way of measuring whether or not you're getting to where you want to be."
Frustrating (33) means **(a)** amusing **(b)** bad **(c)** discouraging **(d)** unexpected.

THINKING IT OVER

1. What makes a television news show good?
2. Do you watch a news show now and then? What do you like about it? What do you dislike?
3. How does Bryant Gumbel provide a good role model for all young people?
4. In what ways is a television news show better than a newspaper? In what ways is a newspaper better?
5. A program like *60 Minutes* or *20/20* calls itself a "news magazine." It tries to give the background of the news. Have you ever watched one of these programs or another like it? Do you think such programs are successful? Give your opinion.

ANOTHER LOOK AT THE QUOTATION

Consider the postage stamp, my son.
Its usefulness consists in its ability to
stick to one thing until it gets there.
JOSH BILLINGS

1. Explain the quotation in your own words.
2. Is the tone of this quotation serious or humorous? Explain.
3. Did Bryant Gumbel stick to his job until he got to the *Today* show? Did he prove that a person can handle several different kinds of jobs? Explain.

WORDS AT YOUR SERVICE—EXPLANATION

Bryant has a lively personality. In many ways he is an *extravert*—that is, he usually doesn't keep things locked inside him. (32)

If *extravert* is a new word for you, don't worry. It's quickly explained. An *extravert* is someone who doesn't keep things locked inside. Often a writer will give a convenient explanation of a word for the reader. This usually happens when a word is used that the reader might not be familiar with. Look for such clues in your own reading.

Study the following sentences and then guess at the meaning of each *italicized* word. Use all of the sentence to help you.

EXAMPLE

My brother Ed has an *extensive* knowledge of American history. He has read widely and spent many years learning about the American story.
Extensive means (a) slight (b) thorough (c) one-sided (d) recent.
If Ed has read widely and spent many years studying, his knowledge must be (b) *thorough.*

1. We think the new restaurant in town will *thrive*. It should be successful.

Thrive means **(a)** disappear **(b)** get many times as large **(c)** do well **(d)** close on weekends.

2. The Hudson River is easily *navigable* to Albany, New York. Ships can sail to that port with ease.
Navigable means **(a)** broad but very shallow **(b)** deep but very narrow **(c)** closed to traffic **(d)** safe for a ship.

3. The runner had a *woeful* expression. He was sorrowful because he had lost the race by tripping only a hundred yards from the finish line.
Woeful means **(a)** sad **(b)** interested **(c)** humorous **(d)** unfriendly.

4. Our stamp club is taking part in the *exposition*. We are displaying many sheets from our collections.
Exposition means **(a)** musical performance **(b)** exhibition **(c)** parade **(d)** stage production.

5. Melanie's ideas were *controversial*. We debated them all afternoon.
Controversial means **(a)** causing people to argue **(b)** without color **(c)** well stated **(d)** soon forgotten.

COMPLETING AN OUTLINE

The article on Bryant Gumbel might be outlined in the following way. Five outline items have been omitted. Test your understanding of the structure of the article by following the directions after the outline.

    I. Television news
       A. Local news shows
       B.
       C. Network morning shows
       D. Opening on the *Today* show
       E. Selection of Bryant Gumbel

II. Bryant Gumbel's preparation
   A.
   B. Co-host of the NFL-NBC show
   C. Co-host of *Grandstand*
   D. Sportscaster on *Today*

III. Gumbel and *Today*
   A. Member of three-person team
   B. Member of two-person team
   C. Popularity
   D. Travels
   E.

IV. Gumbel's origins
   A. Birth in New Orleans
   B.
   C. Graduation from Bates College
   D. Importance of father

V. Gumbel the man
   A. Self-confidence
   B. Lively personality
   C.
   D. Attitude toward his job

Fill in the items omitted from the outline. Correctly match the items in column A with the outline numbers in column B, which show where each item belongs in the outline.

A	B
1. Love of family	a. I. B.
2. Network evening shows	b. II. A.
3. Prizes	c. III. E.
4. Editor of *Black Sports*	d. IV. B
5. Childhood in Chicago	e. V. C.

GEORGE LUCAS AND STEVEN SPIELBERG:
Masters of Fantasy

Your time is limited, but your imagination isn't.

STANFORD LEE

Two great films appeared in the same year, 1977: *Star Wars* and *Close Encounters of the Third Kind*. Both are science fiction. Both deal with beings from other worlds. Each was directed by a young movie genius. George Lucas directed *Star Wars*. Steven Spielberg directed *Close Encounters of the Third Kind*. Both men were named for an Academy Award.

The two films are alike in many ways. Both depend on dazzling special effects. Both *stimulate* the imagination and take movie audiences into new worlds. Both have attractive characters.

There are differences. *Star Wars* takes place in a galaxy far away and long ago. *Close Encounters of the Third Kind* takes place on Earth in the present. *Star Wars* emphasizes the fight between good and evil, between forces of *liberation* and forces of slavery. *Close Encounters of the Third Kind* suggests that good, not evil, is the major force in the universe.

Lucas and Spielberg are close friends. They help each other. They sometimes work on the same film. They joined to create *Raiders of the Lost Ark*. Each of them added a special quality to make this film one of the most financially successful movies of all time.

Though they came together on *Raiders of the Lost Ark,* they arrived from somewhat different directions.

George Lucas was born on May 14, 1944, in Modesto, California. As he was growing up, he did not plan to become a film director. He dreamed of racing motorcars. As he used to drive up and down McHenry Avenue in Modesto, he would picture himself driving home after winning one of the big races.

This dream was smashed three days before his high school graduation. He was in an accident that crushed his lungs. He lingered between life and death for three days. He had to stay in the hospital for three months.

After he gave up his racing dream, he hoped to become an artist. His parents would not send him to art school, so he went to Modesto Junior College. While there he became interested in film work. This new interest changed his life. He and a friend experimented with trick photography. His imagination was captured by this new field of interest.

A friend from his racing days, Haskell Wexler, was a skilled cameraman. Wexler encouraged Lucas and helped him gain admission to the film department at the University of Southern California. At the college Lucas made a short science-fiction film that won first prize at a film festival.

Francis Ford Coppola, director of *The Godfather,* was also interested in Lucas. He got Warner Brothers to sign a contract with him. Lucas developed his short science-fiction film into a full-length feature, *THX 1138.* This movie did not make much money, but it did show what Lucas was able to do. It looked ahead to the very successful *Star Wars.*

People who thought Lucas could handle only science fiction were soon proved wrong. Lucas next directed a low-budget movie that became a big hit. For this movie Lucas went back to his boyhood experiences in Modesto. Called *American Graffiti,* it tells the story of four adolescent boys. The action takes place on a summer night in 1962. The boys have just graduated from high school. The Viet-Nam War is heating up, and the future is uncertain. Some graduates are leaving for college. Others are going into military service.

American Graffiti has very little plot, but it has warm characters in a believable setting. Unlike his later, more expensive films, it was shot in 28 days on a *shoestring* budget of only $780,000! It featured many fine young actors, such as Ronny Howard, Richard Dreyfuss, Cindy

Williams, and Suzanne Somers. It was named for a number of Academy Awards and established George Lucas as a leading director. The movie made it possible for Lucas to make *Star Wars*.

When Lucas was seriously injured in the automobile accident, he developed a religious faith that helped pull him through. This faith appears as the Force in the *Star Wars* films. It is the Force that helps Luke Skywalker and his friends in their battle against the evil Empire.

In the *Star Wars* films, Lucas has created many characters to identify with. There are human characters, like Luke, Princess Leia, and Han Solo. And of course there is the evil Darth Vader. But there also are nonhuman characters that audiences love. There are two robots named *Artoo Detoo* and *See Threepio*. While Yoda the Jedi master is nonhuman, he is superhuman in his powers. All these characters come to life under Lucas's skilled direction. Of *Star Wars,* film critic John Culhane said, "It was full of humanity, too, although many of the characters were creations of special-effects workshops."

Many years ago Lucas outlined plans for a number of pictures that would be part of the *Star Wars* series. Some have already appeared. *Star Wars,* of course, is the first. *The Empire Strikes Back* moves the story on in a brilliant *sequel,* a follow-up with the same excitement. *The Return of the Jedi,* the third film, *retains* the favorite characters and introduces new ones. It continues the breathless special effects that kept audiences watching in the previous two films.

Then Lucas had an idea for a movie that used techniques of an earlier time. In the early days of film, serials were popular. Every Saturday an episode of a popular serial would be shown. At the end of every episode, the hero or heroine would be placed in a dangerous position. Escape seemed impossible. The audience had to "wait till next week" to see how the lead characters escaped.

"Why not use this device in a movie?" Lucas discussed this idea with Spielberg. The two joined forces for *Raiders of the Lost Ark* and its sequel, *Indiana Jones and the Temple of Doom*. Both movies featured Harrison Ford as Indiana Jones.

How did Steven Spielberg first gain success? He traveled a different road from Lucas. Spielberg was born on December 18, 1947, in Cincinnati, Ohio. He was the eldest of four children. His father was an electrical engineer and computer expert. His mother had been a concert pianist. As his father changed jobs, Steven lived in a variety of places. Steven was active in Scouting and Little League baseball. But his heart was in film making.

George Lucas came to films after losing his dream of becoming a race-car driver. Steven Spielberg started earlier. As a child, he was the official family photographer. He used his father's 8-mm movie camera to record family activities. He was not satisfied with just taking the pictures as people waved at the camera. He tried different camera angles. He tried technical tricks. He even created some short horror films starring his three younger sisters. "I killed them all several times," he told one reporter.

His family restricted his moviegoing. The first movie Spielberg saw was a circus movie, *The Greatest Show on Earth*. He was five or six at the time. In an interview Spielberg told of this important event in his life.

"My father said, 'It's going to be bigger than you, but that's all right. The people in it are going to be up on a screen and they can't get out at you.' But there they were up on that screen *and they were getting out at me*. I guess ever since then I've wanted to try to involve the audience as much as I can, so they no longer think they're sitting in an audience."

In high school Spielberg made many short films. He kept alive his interest in science fiction. He spent hours gazing through his homemade reflecting telescope.

While in college Spielberg went to the movies often. He bluffed his way onto movie sets and watched the great directors. He made a short film that was noticed by film executives. He was signed to a seven-year contract to direct television movies. One of these full-length television movies was *Duel*. It told the story of a hair-raising pursuit. It won several major foreign awards.

Spielberg's first big break was *Jaws*. This film about a killer shark was an instant success. But that success wasn't easy. While making the film, he faced problems of every kind. The weather was often bad. Trouble with workers arose at times. The people living on Martha's Vineyard were often bothered by the crowds of film people. There were technical problems with the mechanical sharks. Though the film was due to be finished in ten weeks, the filming dragged on into late September.

At first, the film seemed a financial disaster. It went over double its original budget. At one point Spielberg was almost fired. But after release, the film soon proved itself a financial winner. The public enjoyed being frightened by the great white shark. The critics admired the camera work.

Film critic Gary Arnold expressed the view of many critics. "There has never been an adventure-thriller quite as terrifying yet enjoyable as *Jaws,* and it should set the standard in its field for many years to come."

Lucas's *American Graffiti* helped pave the way for *Star Wars*. Spielberg's *Jaws* paved the way for *Close Encounters of the Third Kind*. For this great film, Spielberg gathered many excellent artists. Joe Alves was the art director. Douglas Trumbull was the special-effects expert. John Williams composed the music. Richard Dreyfuss, who had starred in *American Graffiti* and *Jaws,* played the leading role.

Most viewers of *Close Encounters of the Third Kind*

were dazzled by the thirty minute climax, as a gigantic spaceship filled the screen with light. Critics mentioned the "breathless sense of wonder" that Spielberg managed to communicate.

Star Wars and *Close Encounters of the Third Kind* were released in the same year. People made comparisons, but Spielberg thinks the films are quite different. This is how he explained the differences.

"*Close Encounters* is an earthbound movie. Its roots are in the familiar routine of suburban life. *Star Wars* is a beautiful, enchanting space opera—a fantasy. . . . I wanted people to walk out [of *Close Encounters*] with more questions than they had when they walked in. I wanted them to consider the possibility that we are not alone in the universe, that the stars are not simply a kind of *nocturnal* wallpaper to be viewed indifferently. People should enjoy looking up at night, exercising their imaginations a little more."

Spielberg continued in this direction with the highly successful *E.T.* In this movie a creature from outer space wins the hearts of all viewers. To Spielberg the universe is not a terrifying place.

The careers of Lucas and Spielberg have run parallel courses. Now and then their courses come together, as they did in the Indiana Jones movies. Their ideas stir each other on to greater heights. Perhaps Lucas would not have been as great without Spielberg. Perhaps Spielberg would not have been as great without Lucas. Both careers hold great promise.

UNDERSTANDING WHAT YOU HAVE READ

Finding Another Title

1. Another good title for this selection might be (a) A Breakthrough in Films (b) How to Become a Director in Hollywood (c) Two Young Geniuses of the Films (d) How George Lucas Met Steven Spielberg.

Getting the Main Idea

2. Three qualities most helpful in directing well are (a) experience, imagination, and courage (b) luck, money, and worry (c) youth, eagerness, and unwillingness to take chances (d) early training in films, a sense of humor, and physical strength.

Finding Details

3. A film that Lucas and Spielberg worked closely together on is (a) *E.T.* (b) *American Graffiti* (c) *Duel* (d) *Raiders of the Lost Ark.*
4. Francis Ford Coppola (a) directed *E.T.* (b) helped George Lucas (c) was a special-effects expert (d) is related to Steven Spielberg.
5. *THX 1138* is an early film by (a) Steven Spielberg (b) Francis Ford Coppola (c) Ronny Howard (d) George Lucas.

6. A very successful low-budget film is (a) *Raiders of the Lost Ark* (b) *E.T.* (c) *American Graffiti* (d) *Star Wars.*

7. *The Empire Strikes Back* is a follow-up film to (a) *Close Encounters of the Third Kind* (b) *Star Wars* (c) *E.T.* (d) *Indiana Jones and the Temple of Doom.*

8. *Jaws* was filmed mostly in (a) Modesto, California (b) Cincinnati, Ohio (c) a studio at the University of Southern California (d) Martha's Vineyard.

9. The film that went over double its original budget is (a) *The Empire Strikes Back* (b) *Jaws* (c) *The Godfather* (d) *The Greatest Show on Earth.*

10. Two films that Richard Dreyfuss appeared in are (a) *Close Encounters of the Third Kind* and *American Graffiti* (b) *Jaws* and *Raiders of the Lost Ark* (c) *THX 1138* and *American Graffiti* (d) *Star Wars* and *The Empire Strikes Back.*

Making Inferences

11. Financial backers were willing to put up money for *Star Wars* because (a) George Lucas matched every cent with money of his own (b) *American Graffiti* had been such a success (c) Steven Spielberg gave the project his blessing (d) Lucas had already produced the successful *Empire Strikes Back.*

12. John Culhane (44) believes that the make-believe characters in *Star Wars* are (a) ugly (b) silly (c) shallow (d) like humans.

13. *The Greatest Show on Earth* taught Steven Spielberg (a) how to get audiences involved in a picture (b) the importance of getting stars for a movie (c) the value of having a good sound track (d) how to contact important producers.

14. At the time Steven Spielberg was experimenting with films as a child, (a) his parents tried to discourage him (b) his sisters refused to help him (c) George Lucas was dreaming of becoming a race-car driver (d) George Lucas had already been hired by a studio.

15. Spielberg and Lucas often call upon actors Harrison Ford and Richard Dreyfuss because (a) they were all good friends in high school (b) the actors shared in the writing of the movies (c) they were experienced actors in hit films (d) the actors do not command big salaries.

Predicting What Happens Next

16. After the successful Indiana Jones pictures, Spielberg and Lucas most likely (a) continued to give each other ideas (b) exchanged writers (c) gave up directing for acting (d) jealously decided to go their own ways.

Deciding on the Order of Events

17. The following events are scrambled. Arrange them in proper order, as they happened. Use letters only.

(a) George Lucas attends the University of Southern California.
(b) Steven Spielberg is born in Cincinnati, Ohio.
(c) Steven Spielberg directs *Close Encounters of the Third Kind.*
(d) George Lucas is born in Modesto, California.

Inferring Tone

18. In describing the effect of *The Greatest Show on Earth,* Spielberg (45) suggests a feeling of (a) boredom (b) irritation (c) excitement (d) criticism.

Separating Facts from Opinions

For each of the following, tell whether the statement is a fact *(F)* or an opinion *(O)*.
19. In many ways, Lucas is a better director than Spielberg.
20. Of the two Indiana Jones pictures mentioned, *Raiders of the Lost Ark* is the more believable.

Understanding Words from Context

21. Both of these exciting films *stimulate* the imagination.

Stimulate (42) means **(a)** stir up **(b)** calm **(c)** replace **(d)** make a record of.

22. *Star Wars* emphasizes the fight between good and evil, between forces of *liberation* and forces of slavery.
   Liberation (42) means **(a)** joy **(b)** freedom **(c)** conquest **(d)** excitement.

23. Unlike his later, more expensive films, *American Graffiti* was shot in 28 days on a *shoestring* budget of only $780,000!
   In this sentence *shoestring* (43) means **(a)** tied up **(b)** well planned **(c)** small **(d)** oversized.

24. *The Return of the Jedi*, the third film, *retains* the favorite characters and introduces new ones.
   Retains (44) means **(a)** describes **(b)** makes fun of **(c)** compares **(d)** keeps.

25. Spielberg wanted people to understand that the stars are not simply a kind of *nocturnal* wallpaper.
   Nocturnal (47) means occurring **(a)** every day **(b)** weekly **(c)** at night **(d)** often.

THINKING IT OVER

1. Do you enjoy stories of imagination? Retell one of your favorites.
2. When you go to the movies, do you look for realism or escape? Explain.
3. Have you ever seen a Lucas or Spielberg movie? Did you enjoy it? Tell about it.
4. Someone has said that special effects are not enough. We need stories with interesting characters. Do you agree? Explain.

5. How did the early life of both Spielberg and Lucas affect their later lives?
6. People seldom gain success on their own. Somewhere along the line they are helped by others. How were Lucas and Spielberg both helped by others?
7. Sometimes bad events have good results. How did Lucas's accident have a happy result?

ANOTHER LOOK AT THE QUOTATION

> *Your time is limited, but your*
> *imagination isn't.*
> STANFORD LEE

1. Explain the quotation in your own words.
2. Do you agree with the quotation? Tell why or why not.
3. Scientists believe that we have a left brain and a right brain. The left brain controls the right side of the body. The right brain controls the left side of the body. The left brain is the businesslike brain. It is generally responsible for language, speech, and thinking. The left brain is your good friend, helping you follow directions and getting you to school on time.

   The right brain has a different set of abilities. It helps you think, too, but in creative ways. It is not skilled in language, but it can help with problems that stump the left brain. It has a different kind of understanding

   Your daily existence depends upon the left brain. It is sober, reliable, steady, and not too surprising. But your right brain adds color to your life. Some of your hunches, guesses, and sudden flashes of understanding come from the right brain. Your daydreams and your imaginative ideas also come from the right brain.

When Stanford Lee says your imagination isn't limited, what is he saying about the powers of your right brain?

WORDS AT YOUR SERVICE—SYNONYMS

The Empire Strikes Back moves the story on in a brilliant *sequel,* a follow-up with the same excitement. (44)

If you were not sure about the word *sequel,* you could have guessed the meaning from the context. In the second chapter you learned that an entire sentence can give you a clue to the meaning of a word. Here you don't need all of the sentence. The word *sequel* is followed immediately by another word that means the same thing: *follow-up.* This word, called a *synonym,* provides a clue to the meaning of *sequel* and adds another bit of information.

To make their meaning clearer, writers sometimes give synonyms. One of the synonyms is usually easier than the other. This helps you understand the less familiar word.

Study the following sentences and then guess the meaning of each *italicized* word. Use the entire sentence to help you.

EXAMPLE

Princess Leia's situation was dangerous, but Luke Skywalker was in a more *perilous* trap.
Perilous means **(a)** hazardous **(b)** relaxing **(c)** interesting **(d)** secure.
Perilous is clearly linked with its synonym *dangerous*. The correct answer is **(a)** *hazardous*.

1. The controls of the spaceship were *mangled,* damaged almost beyond repair.
   Mangled means **(a)** studied **(b)** in good shape **(c)** ruined **(d)** glowing.
2. When I yearn for chocolate, I especially *crave* chocolate cake.
   Crave means **(a)** desire **(b)** bake **(c)** sample **(d)** try.
3. The student *browsed* through the magazine and looked over a book or two.
   Browsed means **(a)** rushed **(b)** passed **(c)** stumbled **(d)** glanced.
4. The lawyer for the newspaper gave a heated, *fervent* speech on the need to protect the First Amendment.
   Fervent means **(a)** incorrect **(b)** excited **(c)** dull **(d)** clever.
5. Charles *readily* agreed to the new plan, willingly giving up the idea he had presented.
   Readily means **(a)** freely **(b)** unhappily **(c)** humorously **(d)** unexpectedly.

ANOTHER LOOK

HOW MUCH DO YOU REMEMBER?

1. Bill Cosby was once **(a)** a fine athlete **(b)** president of NBC **(c)** a friend of Rosalyn Sussman Yalow **(d)** a practicing lawyer.
2. Rosalyn Sussman Yalow is **(a)** a scientist at Yale University **(b)** a strong supporter of women's rights **(c)** a novelist as well as a scientist **(d)** the mother of five children.
3. Bryant Gumbel was both a **(a)** sportscaster and newscaster **(b)** weather person and newscaster **(c)** financial reporter and newscaster **(d)** sportscaster and weather person.
4. Spielberg and Lucas worked most closely together on **(a)** *Star Wars* **(b)** *Close Encounters of the Third Kind* **(c)** *The Greatest Show on Earth* **(d)** *Raiders of the Lost Ark.*
5. Rosalyn Sussman Yalow won a Nobel Prize for **(a)** literature **(b)** economics **(c)** medicine **(d)** furthering the cause of peace.
6. Cosby's new show did well largely because the characters were **(a)** silly **(b)** real **(c)** friends of Cosby **(d)** created by a doctor.
7. The person who had a chance because of the transfer of another is **(a)** Rosalyn Sussman Yalow **(b)** Bryant Gumbel **(c)** Steven Spielberg **(d)** Bill Cosby.

8. The two people who dealt in science fiction and the world of imagination are (a) Rosalyn Sussman Yalow and George Lucas (b) Bryant Gumbel and Steven Spielberg (c) Bill Cosby and Bryant Gumbel (d) Steven Spielberg and George Lucas.
9. The person who has not depended on movies or television for a living is (a) Bryant Gumbel (b) George Lucas (c) Bill Cosby (d) Rosalyn Sussman Yalow.
10. The person who won an award for talking with leaders of Soviet Russia is (a) Bill Cosby (b) George Lucas (c) Edward R. Murrow (d) Bryant Gumbel.

WHAT IS YOUR OPINION?

1. Which person in this unit seems to you to have done the most for other people? Explain your choice.
2. Many famous people made their mark when they were young. Which persons in this unit made important contributions while still young?
3. What qualities are needed for those who wish to break new ground?
4. Have you ever been discouraged from doing something because people said, "It won't work"? Tell about your experience.
5. Why do people try to imitate success? Can you mention television shows that tried to imitate other successful ones?
6. How would you define an *original?* Why is it so hard to be original in television?

THE QUOTATION AND THE UNIT

> *If a man does not keep pace with his companions, perhaps it is because he hears a different drummer. Let him step to the music that he hears, however measured or far away.*
>
> HENRY DAVID THOREAU

1. Explain the quotation in your own words.
2. When is it a good idea to follow the crowd and do what the crowd is doing? Explain. When is it a bad idea to follow the crowd? How can you tell the difference?
3. Have you ever "broken new ground" and started something new? Tell about your experience.
4. "Be yourself!" Is that always good advice? Explain.

UNIT 2

PROVING LEADERSHIP

No amount of study or learning will make a man a leader unless he has the natural qualities of one.

SIR ARCHIBALD WAVELL

There is an old Yugoslav proverb that says, "If you wish to know what a man is, place him in authority." Leadership may be a natural gift, but people do not always use it for the good. One of the most dangerous people of modern times was Adolf Hitler. He was a most effective leader, but his goals were evil.

The four subjects in this unit are examples of good leaders.

59

They prove that leadership is important in many different fields. Henry Cisneros is effective in city politics. Patricia Roberts Harris was effective in national politics. Both helped the people. Both were courageous leaders who sometimes took unpopular stands. They would agree with Arnold Glasow, who said, "Candidates who straddle important issues are taken for a ride."

Sequoyah and Joe Montana are quite different. Sequoyah gave his Cherokee nation a written language. It can be said that he led his nation into the modern world. Joe Montana proved again and again his leadership on the football field.

These are four different personalities, but they are all examples of effective leadership used for good.

HENRY CISNEROS:
Champion of the Cities

America's cities are the windows through which the world looks at American society.

HENRY CISNEROS

"Who is Henry Cisneros?"
It was the summer of 1984. The presidential race was heating up. Walter Mondale would be the Democratic candidate to run against Ronald Reagan. Who would be his running mate? Many names were mentioned. Many persons from all over the United States were *summoned* to a meeting.

Among the persons called was Henry Cisneros, mayor of San Antonio. San Antonio is the tenth largest city in the United States, but Cisneros was new to national politics. He was well loved and well known in the Southwest. Elsewhere in the country he was largely unknown.

Cisneros was the first Hispanic mayor of a large American city. This fact brought him to Mondale's attention. Mondale considered the need for a balanced ticket.

"Cisneros will be the best choice to run with Mondale," said many advisers. For a while it looked as though Cisneros might be chosen. Finally, though, Walter Mondale chose Geraldine Ferraro, the first woman to run for vice president. But the name of Cisneros would not be forgotten.

Henry Cisneros stands out among politicians. He is a man with a special vision and the energy to make the dream real. He is as *energetic* as a bee in a flower garden. He is a born leader. Yet he is a modest man who lives simply.

Cisneros first ran for mayor of San Antonio in 1979. He won 63 percent of the vote. When he ran again in 1983, he won an *astounding* 94.2 percent of the vote. In most elections a 60 percent share of the vote is thought to be a "landslide." Cisneros's margin of victory was almost unheard of in American political history. People of every race and religion had voted for him.

Why did Cisneros win the approval of the citizens of San Antonio? They realized that Cisneros was good for the city. He took on the city's problems with enthusiasm. He set up a plan and followed it.

Cisneros has studied the strengths and problems of American cities. He believes he has a plan for the future. In 1982 Cisneros delivered a famous talk to the City Club of New York. The speech was considered one of the most important of the year. In the speech he outlined the history of American cities. He discussed their current problems and then looked to the future. He made some of the following points.

Cities are central to American life. Their art galleries and museums show us our artistic heritage and present new art forms. Cities help change the way we look at life.

New communication ideas are developed in the cities. Great centers of learning provide experimentation and research. Large medical centers lead the way in health care.

Cities have always played an important role in the economic life of the nation. The tiny villages where the early settlers traded their goods have become the giant cities of today. Those villages were the centers of economic life. So are the cities today. By 1690 most American colonists were city dwellers. A higher number of Americans than Britons then lived in cities.

In the early colonies six great seaports became centers of economic activity. In New England, Newport and especially Boston welcomed ships with goods from Europe. By 1700, Boston was the third largest seaport in the English-speaking world. In the Middle colonies, New York, Philadelphia, and Baltimore were *hubs* of activity. In the Southern colonies, Charleston was an important seaport.

As the country grew, other great cities were founded. Not all of these were seaports. San Francisco and Los Angeles were on the ocean, but inland cities also flourished. San Antonio was far from seaports, but it was an important trading center. Chicago was an important rail center. Kansas City was the meeting point for cattle drives. Cincinnati's growth depended on the steamboat. Every great American city filled a special need.

Cities are not all growing at the same rate. In fact, in some cities the population is actually declining. In others it is growing by leaps and bounds. Sunbelt cities like San Antonio, Houston, and Phoenix are attracting more and more people.

Some cities depend heavily on a single industry. Detroit, for example, depends on the automobile industry. A major slowdown in auto sales hurts Detroit severely.

In every city there are large numbers of people with low incomes. Many mayors spend a great deal of time on plans like welfare and unemployment relief. These are important, of course. But Cisneros thinks these programs provide only temporary help. He wants to get to the root of the problem. He wants to cure the disease, not just treat the symptoms.

"Let them vote with their feet." This is the negative advice sometimes given to mayors of troubled cities. This advice means, "If there is high unemployment, let the unemployed move to other cities or towns. There are always jobs somewhere in the country."

This advice is not practical. It is difficult for whole families to *uproot* themselves and move to other places. The unemployed may not have the special skills needed for the jobs that are still open. Then, too, the city they leave behind may have other serious problems.

Cisneros does not believe that this kind of thinking solves any problems. He feels that the cities can deal with their problems by making special efforts. If cities don't send their unemployed elsewhere, what can they do?

"Create more jobs," says Cisneros. This is Cisneros's dream.

That solution is more easily said than done. It calls for a lot of work. It demands sacrifice on the part of some people. It needs an enthusiastic mayor to lead the way. It also needs a sympathetic national government and a partnership between business and government.

Not all cities are suited for all industries. Each city must know its own special strengths. It must then start educating and training workers.

Cisneros thinks there are five key areas in the new technologies. These are improved industrial processes, communications, aerospace, agriculture, and medicine. He wants to aid businesses. He has created a *Blueprint* showing how San Antonio can help in each area. He has also shown how San Antonio's closeness to Mexico can be a help.

Cisneros sees San Antonio as a city ready for the industries of the future. These high-technology industries will provide an increasing number of jobs. He thinks that the people living in San Antonio can fill those jobs.

Cisneros doesn't expect miracles. He believes in training people. For example, he persuaded officials of the University of Texas to add an engineering school to its San Antonio branch. He draws modern industries to San Antonio, but he knows these industries will need trained people.

He has drawn firms with modern names like *Control Data, Micro-Devices,* and *Sprague Electric.* He thinks drawing industry to the city one of his most important jobs. San Antonio is growing rapidly. But the growth has been planned.

Cisneros has made industries change their view of the Mexican American worker. He has proved that these workers work hard and well and are loyal. Mexican Americans have proved that they can get ahead in this new age. They have made clear that any minority, given training and help, can take an honored place in American industrial society.

What kind of person is Henry Cisneros? Three words best describe him: *brilliant, modest,* and *sincere.* He puts on no airs. In a news report, Marshall Ingwerson wrote, "Mayor Cisneros is simply 'Henry' to virtually everyone from leading lawyers to the local bookstore staff."

Cisneros was born in 1947. He earned a bachelor of arts degree from Texas A & M University in 1968. He soon showed an interest in government. He became administrative assistant in the office of the city manager of San Antonio. He went to Washington in 1970 as an assistant to the executive vice president of the National League of Cities.

Cisneros held other jobs before returning to San Antonio. In August 1974 he became a faculty member of the University of Texas at San Antonio. After he became mayor, he continued teaching. The salary of mayor is too low to live on, so the mayor must have other sources of income.

There were many influences on Henry Cisneros. One of the strongest was his grandfather, Henry Romulo Munguia, who came to the United States from Mexico. Another was his father, George, who was a colonel in the United States Army.

Cisneros's interest in the problems of cities came about partly by accident. While at Texas A & M, he was chosen to attend the Student Conference on National Affairs in Washington, D.C.

As he later said, "It was a very heady and *exhilarating* experience to be in the nation's capital, meeting people from all parts of the country and discussing the great events and issues of the day."

On the plane home, he read an article about the problems of cities. This article, by Daniel Patrick Moynihan, gave Cisneros much to think about. As the reporter Scott

Bennett said, "The two events—visiting Washington and reading the article—marked the beginning of Cisneros' long love affair with government and cities."

It was a fortunate day for America. Henry Cisneros is helping us take a great step toward solving the problems of cities. In time his influence will become even greater.

UNDERSTANDING WHAT YOU HAVE READ

Finding Another Title

1. Another good title for this selection might be **(a)** San Antonio, City of the Future **(b)** Henry Cisneros and His Dream for American Cities **(c)** The Place of San Antonio Among Great American Cities **(d)** The First Term of Mayor Cisneros.

Getting the Main Idea

2. Henry Cisneros **(a)** is not afraid to try new ideas to solve the problems of cities **(b)** does not think welfare an important problem in most cities **(c)** won the election for mayor by a landslide **(d)** was once thought of as a vice presidential candidate.

Finding Details

3. Cisneros won 94.2 percent of the vote in **(a)** 1968 **(b)** 1979 **(c)** 1983 **(d)** 1984.

4. In 1700 the third largest seaport in the English-speaking world was **(a)** Newport **(b)** Boston **(c)** New York **(d)** Baltimore.

5. All of the following are mentioned as seaport cities EXCEPT **(a)** Boston **(b)** Providence **(c)** New York **(d)** Charleston.

6. Cincinnati is associated with **(a)** railroads **(b)** stockyards **(c)** the steamboat **(d)** aerospace.

7. A city that depends heavily on one industry is **(a)** Detroit **(b)** Phoenix **(c)** Philadelphia **(d)** San Francisco.

8. *Control Data* is **(a)** the name of a firm **(b)** a title of a book **(c)** the title of a speech by Cisneros **(d)** a new way of handling a computer.

9. The Student Conference on National Affairs was held in **(a)** San Antonio **(b)** Dallas **(c)** Miami **(d)** Washington.

10. Daniel Patrick Moynihan influenced Cisneros **(a)** by a television speech **(b)** in private conversation **(c)** through a close friend **(d)** by an article.

Making Inferences

11. Walter Mondale most likely chose Geraldine Ferraro as his running mate because **(a)** he disliked Cisneros **(b)** she had run for the Senate earlier **(c)** he tossed a coin **(d)** he thought she would win many votes among women.

12. The vote in the second election that Cisneros won suggests that **(a)** many people came out to vote **(b)** Cisneros did many good things in his first term **(c)** he was elected solely because of the Mexican-American vote **(d)** the way of counting the votes was not fair.

13. Cisneros's talk to the City Club of New York probably **(a)** was written by an assistant **(b)** was not sincere **(c)** got national attention **(d)** was soon forgotten.

14. Cities like San Antonio, Houston, and Phoenix are probably growing rapidly because of their **(a)** mild climate **(b)** nearness to San Francisco **(c)** high taxes **(d)** large airports.

15. Cisneros's *Blueprint* is probably **(a)** written in Spanish **(b)** a plan setting forth temporary solutions **(c)** given to industries that might settle in San Antonio **(d)** the United States government's plan for the development of cities.

Predicting What Happens Next

16. After Cisneros leaves office as mayor of San Antonio, the city will probably **(a)** give up the plans of Henry Cisneros **(b)** make a rule against three-time mayors **(c)** begin to lose population **(d)** continue the policies of its popular mayor.

Deciding on the Order of Events

17. The following events are scrambled. Arrange them in proper order, as they happened. Use letters only.
    (a) Cisneros meets Walter Mondale and is considered as a vice presidential candidate.
    (b) Henry Romulo Munguia comes to the United States.
    (c) Cisneros gets a bachelor of arts degree from Texas A & M.
    (d) San Antonio elects Cisneros mayor for the first time.

Inferring Tone

18. The tone of Cisneros's comment about his trip to the Student Conference on National Affairs (66) was (a) bored (b) happy (c) enthusiastic (d) doubtful.

Separating Facts from Opinions

For each of the following, tell whether the statement is a fact (*F*) or an opinion (*O*).

19. Cisneros won the election of 1979 with 63 percent of the vote.
20. Kansas City was the meeting point for cattle drives.

Understanding Words from Context

21. Many persons from all over the United States were *summoned* to a meeting.
    Summoned (62) means (a) called (b) taken (c) announced (d) flown.
22. He won an *astounding* 94.2 percent of the vote.
    Astounding (62) means (a) unexpected (b) closely studied (c) easily achieved (d) amazing.
23. New York, Philadelphia, and Baltimore were *hubs* of activity.
    Hubs (63) means (a) industries (b) states (c) centers (d) markets.
24. It is difficult for whole families to *uproot* themselves and move to other places.
    Uproot (64) means (a) destroy (b) displace (c) retain (d) discover.
25. Cisneros said that discussing the great issues of the day "was a very heady and *exhilarating* experience."
    Exhilarating (66) means (a) exciting (b) sad (c) unimportant (d) funny.

THINKING IT OVER

1. Some cities are rebuilding downtown areas and are putting in shopping centers and other attractions. Do you consider this a good idea? Explain.
2. If you were mayor of your own or a nearby city, mention one plan you would introduce to help the city.
3. Should a vice presidential candidate be chosen only on ability, or should his or her vote-getting power also be considered? Explain.
4. Should the national government step in to help cities in trouble? Explain.
5. Many cities have both a mayor and a city manager. The mayor, who is elected by the people, is the boss. The city manager, who is appointed, is responsible for running the day-by-day affairs of city government. The city manager may last through several changes of mayor. Does this seem to you a good idea? Why or why not?

ANOTHER LOOK AT THE QUOTATION

America's cities are the windows through which the world looks at American society.
HENRY CISNEROS

1. Foreigners know more about American cities than they know about the countryside. Why do you think Cisneros compares American cities to windows?
2. How did Henry Cisneros show, by his own actions, how important he considered the problems of cities?
3. From what you have read, do you think San Antonio would probably be a good "window" through which the world might look at America? Explain.

WORDS AT YOUR SERVICE—COMPARISONS

He is as *energetic* as a bee in a flower garden. (62)

If you did not know the word *energetic,* you could have guessed the meaning from the context. The rest of the words in the sentence give clues to the meaning. Here the basic clue is comparison. A bee in a flower garden is extremely busy and lively while gathering pollen. *Energetic,* then, means *marked by effective activity.* An *energetic* person moves about with a lot of useful effort.

Study the following sentences and then guess the meaning of each *italicized* word. Use the entire sentence to help you.

EXAMPLE

The children *frolicked* on the beach like three puppies tumbling on a lawn.
Frolicked means (a) whistled (b) dashed (c) romped (d) fell.
Dogs tumbling on a lawn are playing. The correct answer must be (c) *romped.*

1. The picnickers were as *listless* as a drowsy cat on the hottest day of summer.
   Listless means (a) lacking in energy (b) filled with ambition (c) moving quickly (d) boring.
2. In the salty waters of the Great Salt Lake, Jennifer felt as *buoyant* as a cork.
   Buoyant means *able to* (a) swim (b) sink (c) float (d) dive.
3. The stray horse was as *elusive* as a mosquito in a darkened room.
   Elusive means *hard to* (a) hear (b) shoot (b) win (d) catch.

4. The hikers on the mountain ridge looked as *insignificant* as ants on a brown wall.
   Insignificant means **(a)** strong and imposing **(b)** tiny and unimportant **(c)** bright and shiny **(d)** large but invisible.
5. Merrill was as *agitated* as the sea on a stormy night.
   Agitated means **(a)** wet **(b)** windy **(c)** troubled **(d)** dark.

COMPLETING AN OUTLINE

The article on Henry Cisneros might be outlined in the following way. Five outline items have been omitted. Test your understanding of the structure of the article by following the directions after the outline.

I. Cisneros on the national scene
   A.
   B. Nationwide recognition

II. Cisneros in San Antonio
   A.
   B. Acceptance by voters in all groups
   C. Strong leadership for the future

III. Cisneros's study of the cities' role
   A. Important element in American life
   B.
   C. Development of great cities
   D. Current condition

IV. Cisneros's suggested solutions
    A. Creation of jobs
    B. Sacrifice by citizens
    C. Cooperation of federal government
    D. Determination of cities' strengths
    E.
    F. Increased involvement of minority groups

V. Cisneros the man
    A.
    B. College years
    C. Various jobs held
    D. Interest in problems of cities

Fill in the items omitted from the outline. Correctly match the items in column A with the outline numbers in column B, which show where each item belongs in the outline.

A	B
1. Pleasing personality	a. I. A.
2. Meeting with Walter Mondale	b. II. A.
	c. III. B.
3. Need for job training	d. IV. E.
4. Strong showing in election for mayor	e. V. A.
5. Centers of economic activity	

PATRICIA ROBERTS HARRIS:

Member of the President's Cabinet

*My mother always believed that women
can do whatever they want to do. I grew
up believing that, and I still do.*
PATRICIA ROBERTS HARRIS

The United States government is looked up to by people all over the world. Unlike governments that have experienced sudden changes, it has remained *stable* through depressions and times of unrest. Elections for president have been held even in the middle of terrible wars. The government has worked successfully through two centuries. Governments of other Western democracies have not had so good a record. During the past two centuries, for instance, the governments of France, Germany, and Spain have gone through disastrous changes and *upheavals*.

Why has the government of the United States lasted when most other nations have gone through violent changes? One good reason is the way the government was first set up.

The Founders of our country knew that people are not perfect. They well understood that people with power may abuse that power. They planned to keep any one person from taking over the government. They decided on a separation of powers to keep all leaders accountable to the people. To achieve this goal, they created and approved the Constitution. This remarkable document sets up three branches of government: the legislative, the executive, and the judicial.

Each branch helps to keep the others in check. The division of power can be described in simple terms. The legislative branch makes the laws. The executive branch sees that the laws are carried out. At times, the judicial branch decides whether or not the laws are constitutional. These duties may at times overlap, but the basic principle of separation holds.

The world saw how well the American government works during the Watergate incident. In 1974 President Richard Nixon, the most powerful person in the world at the time, was forced to resign. The Congress had disapproved of his actions. It planned to remove him from office. The president knew the power of the Congress and stepped down before he could be removed.

The executive branch is not all-powerful, but neither are the other two. Presidents can veto legislation and often force their will on the Congress. The Congress may override the veto, but then the judicial branch may step in. The Supreme Court may determine that the law is unconstitutional. And so the separation of powers helps to keep any member or branch of government from becoming too powerful.

Women have come to play a more and more important role in the three branches of government. The legislative branch is made up of the House of Representatives and the Senate. Congress now has many women members. But after 1789 more than a century passed before a woman appeared in Congress. The first woman elected to the House of Representatives was Jeannette Rankin in 1916. The first woman elected to the Senate was Hattie Caraway of Arkansas in 1932.

Major members of the executive branch are the president and the advisers, the Cabinet. Victoria Claflin Woodhull was nominated for president in 1872 by a minority party. In 1984 the Democratic party nominated Geraldine A. Ferraro for vice president. Neither of these candidates was elected, but women have served in the president's Cabinet. The first woman Cabinet member was Frances Perkins, secretary of labor in 1933. The first black woman Cabinet member was Patricia Roberts Harris, secretary of the Department of Housing and Urban Development. (*Urban* means *dealing with cities.*) She was appointed by President Jimmy Carter in 1977.

The judicial branch was the last to admit a woman member to top office. Until 1981 all justices of the Supreme Court had been men. Then in July 1981, Sandra Day O'Connor was chosen by President Ronald Reagan.

She became the first woman member of the United States Supreme Court.

Within each branch of government, strong individuals can make their influence felt. These individuals help to check the power of any one person. By strength of character and good ideas, they provide a balance.

Such a strong person was Patricia Roberts Harris. She was intelligent, courageous, and fair. She played a major role in any group she belonged to. As a member of President Carter's Cabinet from 1977 to 1981, she advised and, sometimes, opposed the president. The mayor of Detroit, Coleman Young, once said, "I don't think there's anybody in the president's Cabinet who will take him on as readily as Pat will." A strong president welcomes intelligent opposition as well as cooperation. Patricia Harris gave Carter all her help and energy.

Patricia Harris's life prepared her for struggle. She was born in 1924, the daughter of a Pullman car waiter. Her childhood in Mattoon, Illinois, was often difficult, stormy, *turbulent*. She felt the stings of prejudice and decided that some day she would help remove that evil. She attended Englewood High School in Chicago and Howard University in Washington, D.C.

Pat Harris graduated with highest honors from Howard. She then earned her master's degree in industrial relations from the University of Chicago. Her next step was graduation from George Washington University's National Law Center. She was first in her class. She was a member of one of the most important honor societies, Phi Beta Kappa. She was also a member of the American Academy of Arts and Sciences.

She became a trial attorney in the Justice Department. She joined the staff of Howard University and was soon promoted to become professor of law and dean of the School of Law.

Her list of achievements doesn't stop! She served on the board of Chase Manhattan Bank, Scott Paper Company, and IBM. She ran a successful law practice with fellow Democrats.

For a long time Patricia Harris was well known in Washington and in legal services elsewhere. She then gained some national attention when she was appointed ambassador to Luxembourg in 1965. She finally became famous when she was appointed secretary of the Department of Housing and Urban Development in 1977 by President Jimmy Carter.

During her years on President Carter's Cabinet, she made many enemies who later became friends. Senator William Proxmire cast the only vote against her selection as secretary of HUD, as the department is frequently called. Later he had only praise for this brave woman who stood up for her beliefs.

She gave freely of her time and energy. She was a *gourmet* cook. But because of her schedule, she had to settle for quickly prepared meals. During her stay as secretary she said, "I haven't done any really serious cooking since I've been secretary of HUD. The first two years, I'd leave here so dead at night I wasn't able to do anything but stumble to the kitchen and follow the line of least resistance in terms of food." She was interested in the arts and often bought opera and symphony tickets. Most of the time she had to give the tickets away.

Patricia Harris assembled a strong staff to help her. She inspired those under her and raised the *morale* of her department. She brought in more minority workers. But she did not blindly select them. They were able people who earned their jobs. She put white workers in black areas and black workers in white areas if they were suited for their tasks.

One of her most experienced staff members was Elmer

Binford. He had worked under five previous secretaries. He said of Harris, "She is one of the most concentrated listeners I've ever met. Frequently when you're talking to a boss, you have to wait until they say their thing before you can say your thing. But with her, she invites comment. She moves her head up and down very encouragingly, like 'please tell me more.' She almost demands that you serve things up to her, even though they might be uncomfortable. She insists on *candor,* because she believes she can get in trouble as much for what she doesn't know as for what she knows. She once told a staffer who challenged her on an issue: 'The day you stop telling me that I'm wrong, out you go.' "

Patricia Roberts Harris left her mark on HUD. Then, in 1979, she was assigned another Cabinet post as secretary of the Department of Health and Human Services. Here again her concern was with people and their welfare.

New presidents choose their own Cabinets. When Ronald Reagan replaced Jimmy Carter, he replaced Patricia Harris in 1981 with Richard S. Schweiker.

But the contributions of Patricia Harris will not be forgotten. Upon her death in 1985, former President Jimmy Carter said that she "was a fine lady and a fine Cabinet officer, sensitive to the needs of others and an able administrator."

She will be missed.

UNDERSTANDING WHAT YOU HAVE READ

Finding Another Title

1. Another good title for this selection might be (a) The Constitution (b) An Able Public Servant (c) Women in Politics (d) How Presidents Choose Cabinet Members.

Getting the Main Idea

2. Patricia Roberts Harris (a) was a fearless, fair, and honest worker (b) disagreed with President Carter (c) was replaced by a man of President Reagan's choice (d) graduated first in her class.

Finding Details

3. The Supreme Court is part of (a) the president's Cabinet (c) the legislative branch (c) the executive branch (d) the judicial branch.
4. Victoria Claflin Woodhull (a) was a senator (b) once ran for the House of Representatives (c) was a secretary of labor (d) was a candidate for president of the United States.
5. Jeannette Rankin (a) was a senator from Arkansas (b) was the first woman member of Congress (c) knew Patricia Harris in law school (d) worked for Mayor Coleman Young.
6. Sandra Day O'Connor was named to the Supreme Court in (a) 1977 (b) 1979 (c) 1981 (d) 1983.
7. Patricia Harris spent her childhood in (a) Chicago (b) Washington (c) Luxembourg (d) Mattoon.

8. Patricia Harris once served on the board of each of these companies EXCEPT (a) General Motors (b) Scott Paper Company (c) IBM (d) Chase Manhattan Bank.
9. Patricia Harris left HUD for (a) the Supreme Court (b) George Washington University's National Law Center (c) the Department of Health and Human Services (d) Luxembourg.
10. All of the following presidents were mentioned in the selection EXCEPT (a) Richard Nixon (b) Gerald Ford (c) Jimmy Carter (d) Ronald Reagan.

Making Inferences

11. The survival of the United States government through two centuries can best be described as (a) not expected (b) not planned (c) remarkable (d) common.
12. By his comment (78), Mayor Coleman Young of Detroit shows that he (a) resented Patricia Harris (b) thought Patricia Harris should not disagree with the president (c) laughed heartily at Patricia Harris's wittiness (d) admired Patricia Harris's courage.
13. As secretary of HUD, Patricia Harris was (a) relaxed and easygoing (b) devoted to her job (c) often late for work (d) unable to get along with her fellow workers.
14. When Patricia Harris told her staff member (80), "Out you go," she was really telling the person to (a) speak frankly (b) get ready to take another job (c) follow orders no matter what (d) be respectful at all times.

15. Patricia Harris was given the post of secretary of Health and Human Services because **(a)** she had done a good job in her previous position **(b)** no one else volunteered for the job **(c)** her term of office would be short **(d)** fellow workers asked that she be assigned.

Predicting What Happens Next

16. After leaving the government in 1981, Patricia Harris probably **(a)** retired to the country **(b)** spent a good part of her time criticizing the man who replaced her **(c)** continued to work hard at whatever job she took on **(d)** put her talents to work as a cook and opened a restaurant.

Deciding on the Order of Events

17. The following events are scrambled. Arrange them in proper order, as they happened. Use letters only.
   (a) Patricia Harris is appointed secretary of Housing and Urban Development.
   (b) Hattie Caraway becomes senator from Arkansas.
   (c) Patricia Harris attends a high school in Chicago.
   (d) Ronald Reagan is elected president.

Inferring Attitude

18. Elmer Binford's attitude (80) toward Patricia Harris is one of **(a)** appreciation for her patience **(b)** doubt about her plans **(c)** irritation at her way of speaking **(d)** fear at her anger.

Separating Facts from Opinions

For each of the following, tell whether the statement is a fact (*F*) or an opinion (*O*).
19. Patricia Roberts Harris did a better job as secretary of HUD than any of those who came before her.
20. In his original attitude toward Patricia Harris, Senator Proxmire was unfair.

Understanding Words from Context

21. Unlike governments that have experienced sudden changes, it has remained *stable* through depressions and periods of social unrest.
    Stable (76) means (a) steady and strong (b) sound but dull (c) rapidly changing (d) interesting and exciting.
22. The governments of France, Germany, and Spain have experienced disastrous *upheavals*.
    Upheavals (76) means (a) severe earthquakes (b) volcanic eruptions (c) frequent floods (d) violent changes.
23. She was a *gourmet* cook, but because of her schedule, she had to settle for quickly prepared meals.
    Gourmet (79) means (a) French (b) expert in foods (c) enthusiastic (d) willing to experiment.
24. She inspired those under her and raised the *morale* of her department.
    Morale (79) means (a) well-being (b) salaries (c) spirit (d) level of honesty.
25. She insists on *candor*, because she believes she can get in trouble as much for what she doesn't know as for what she knows.
    Candor (80) means (a) an open and honest way of speaking (b) respect at all times (c) a willingness to do extra jobs (d) an even temper.

THINKING IT OVER

1. Do you think it is right that a president can be removed from office? Explain.
2. What do you consider were Patricia Harris's strongest qualities as a leader?
3. If you were a boss, would you allow your employees to disagree with you? Why or why not?
4. What is meant by the expression *separation of powers?*
5. How did Patricia Harris's childhood help form her?
6. Should an incoming president keep the Cabinet of the former president? Why or why not?
7. What do you think are the qualities of a good boss?
8. Do Americans sometimes take their blessings for granted? Explain.

ANOTHER LOOK AT THE QUOTATION

> *My mother always believed that*
> *women can do whatever they want to do.*
> *I grew up believing that, and I still do.*
> PATRICIA ROBERTS HARRIS

1. Explain the quotation in your own words.
2. How did Patricia Roberts Harris prove that her mother was right?
3. Do you believe that you can do whatever you want to do if you are self-confident?
4. Soon after the beginning of his second term, President Reagan appointed Aulana Pharis Peters to the Securities and Exchange Commission. She was the first black woman lawyer named to this commission. Would Aulana Peters probably agree with the quotation? Explain.

WORDS AT YOUR SERVICE—SEQUENCE

Her childhood in Mattoon, Illinois, was often difficult, stormy, *turbulent*. (78)

Sometimes a series of connected words provides clues to meaning. *Difficult, stormy,* and *turbulent* are arranged in a sequence, or series. The arrangement suggests an increasing degree of upset from *difficult* to *turbulent*. *Stormy* suggests more of a problem than *difficult*. *Turbulent* suggests even more of a problem. From this sequence, we can guess that *turbulent* means *upset*.

Study the following sentences and then guess the meaning of each *italicized* word. Use sequence clues to help you.

EXAMPLE

When the cake was divided, Mary had a small piece. Gerry had a slightly larger piece. June's was more than *ample*.
Ample means (a) smaller (b) attractive (c) enough (d) tasteless.
Since the sequence tells you that June's piece was the largest, you know that it was more than enough. The answer must be (c) *enough*.

1. Even gentle gorillas somehow look mean, even *ferocious*.
   Ferocious means (a) fierce (b) mild (c) friendly (d) kind.
2. After sunset the evening turned cool. By dawn a biting wind had turned temperatures *frigid*.
   Frigid means (a) a bit chilly (b) mild (c) very cold (d) rainy.

3. After the loss, Brad was more than a little discouraged. He was *dejected*.
   Dejected means **(a)** cheerful **(b)** bored **(c)** active **(d)** depressed.
4. Nedra began her hobby by collecting occasional postage stamps, but she soon began to *hoard* every stamp she could find.
   Hoard means **(a)** soak off envelopes **(b)** keep a hidden supply **(c)** throw away **(d)** destroy.
5. At first the bathers dipped cautious toes into the cold water. Then they completely *submerged* themselves.
   Submerged means **(a)** departed **(b)** went under water **(c)** walked slowly into the water **(d)** shivered without stopping.

SEQUOYAH:
Wizard of the Talking Leaves

*The grand essentials to happiness in
this life are something to do, something
to love, and something to hope for.*
JOSEPH ADDISON

Have you ever thought about the miracle of language? Think for a moment what happens when you speak to a friend. Somehow the rough ideas and pictures inside your head are transmitted to the brain of your friend. You probably won't have exactly the same pictures or ideas. Yet you manage to communicate satisfactorily. If you say, "Please pass the sugar," your friend is not likely to open a window.

Speech arose somewhere in the distant past. It is an ancient human invention. Every group of people has a spoken language; it is *universal*. No matter where the early explorers went, they found people with a well-developed language. None of the languages were simple. Even in tribal societies, the language spoken was *complex*. Spoken language has a long and honorable history.

By comparison, written language is almost a newcomer. Speech comes first. Children learn to speak long before they can read or write. Some tribal communities have a spoken language but not a written language. The opposite is never true. As language student Charles L. Barber writes, "We know of no human society which has a written language without a spoken one." The sign language of the deaf is no exception, for the signs are based on the spoken word and replace speech.

How old is writing? The earliest examples of writing are about 8,000 years old. Tablets of baked clay were found in the ruins of the ancient Chaldean city of Nippur. Later civilizations developed their own form of writing. They used different materials, like stone, clay, palm leaf, and papyrus. Much of the writing has not survived.

A good system of writing is important in the development of civilization. With writing, we can communicate with people far away. We can enter the minds of men and women long dead. We can keep records, transmit important messages, and record history.

There are many interesting chapters in the history of writing, but one chapter stands out. This is the story of the Cherokee Indian Sequoyah* and "The Miracle of the Talking Leaves." Sequoyah's achievement is almost beyond belief. He single-handedly invented a written language for his people. Sequoyah didn't know it couldn't be done. As author C. Fayne Porter says, "How many thousands of years did it take to produce and *refine* the alphabet with which this page is written? Intelligent and well-trained men had already attempted to set the Cherokee tongue into a pattern of letters, but with no success."

How did Sequoyah achieve success? For a time he served in the United States Army during the War of 1812. Sequoyah watched his fellow soldiers closely. They put strange dark marks on a substance no thicker than a leaf. If dropped, this substance, paper, would whirl away in the wind.

The paper was different from a leaf, though. It held people's thoughts. It told of the homesickness of husbands and fathers. It had the power to make other papers come back. The soldiers looked carefully at these papers, or letters, and got all the news of their families. There were no letters for Sequoyah. He had had no word from his family for two years. As Porter says, "None of the Cherokees knew the secret of the talking leaves."

Sequoyah determined to find the secret. He planned to set the Cherokee spoken language into a pattern of letters. Because Sequoyah was not worldly-wise, he was free. He was not afraid to try new things. He had no set ideas. He couldn't speak, read, or write English. But he knew that the talking leaves would help him unite his people.

First he tried picture writing. He invented picture symbols for Cherokee words. He would listen to his friends

---

*si-KWOY-uh

and draw pictures for all the new words he heard. He kept a file of tree bark with all those symbols. This task became the most important in his life. It took all his time and energy. His formerly neat house began to be neglected. His garden became weedy. His friends began to avoid him. Finally, his wife threw all his work into the fire. Scorned and *humiliated,* he left home with his six-year-old daughter, Ah-yoka. He settled in an old, deserted, tumbledown cabin. There he vowed to pick up the task again.

Until then Sequoyah's luck had seemed bad. All his work had been destroyed in a fire. He had to start all over again. Yet this misfortune turned out to be lucky. The luckiest stroke came soon after Sequoyah settled in his new home.

One day he and Ah-yoka were walking along a forest path. "Look!" cried the little girl. "What's that?" A strange flat thing lay half-hidden in the grass. She picked it up and showed it to Sequoyah. It was a book. It held the talking leaves Sequoyah had seen the soldiers use.

Looking back at Sequoyah's life, we realize his wife did him a favor by destroying his picture writing. His original plan might have come to a dead end. Picture writing was not the solution. There was an easier way.

Sequoyah took the book back to his cabin and examined it carefully. There were no pictures in these talking leaves. There were strange black marks very evenly arranged. These marks were combined in ways he didn't understand. He noticed that some marks were repeated. Could there be a sign for each sound in the spoken language?

He noticed that the whole book was made up of only 26 different marks—or letters. How could all those ideas be squeezed into only 26 marks? He had recently drawn hundreds of pictures for things and still had barely scratched the surface. Could everything be put into only 26 marks?

Sequoyah had discovered the alphabet, one of our greatest inventions. Languages which use picture writing need hundreds of thousands of these pictures. Modern Chinese is an example. But languages which use alphabets need only a handful of letters to communicate every imaginable idea.

The beauty of the alphabet is that it relates sounds to symbols. When we see the letter *b* in *bay, able,* or *knob,* we know how to pronounce it. The same letter does many jobs.

There is another kind of written language, called a *syllabary.* This uses written characters, or letters, to represent syllables, like *yo* or *ka.* Because the Cherokee language is so different from English, Sequoyah couldn't easily use all the English letters. He identified 200 sounds in the Cherokee tongue. Since these sounds were really syllables, he made up a written language based on these syllables. He used English letters and combined them with letters of his own to stand for these syllables.

He used his new syllabary to set down his thoughts. Ah-yoka could read back what her father had written. Sequoyah's system worked.

At this time he was probably in his mid-forties. His work was still not recognized by his friends. He was looked upon as an evil spirit, as a man who worked with the devil. He decided to go west.

He and his daughter traveled through the Great Smoky Mountains toward the Mississippi River. They met other Cherokees moving westward, including a widowed woman with an eight-year-old son. Sequoyah married again. His new wife was patient and understanding, and the enlarged family made a new home.

Sequoyah kept working on his syllabary. His stepson and new wife could easily read what he had written. All four tried and tested every new idea. Sequoyah found that he could simplify his syllabary, reducing the 200 forms to 86.

It was time to present his plan to his people. He had to return to those who had laughed at him. He took the long trip back and found a former friend who was now a head man. At first, his friend was not enthusiastic. Sequoyah kept after him and finally got a hearing. Twelve years of his life would soon be tested.

Sequoyah left the room, so that there would be no question of Sequoyah's overhearing. The test was a dramatic one. Ah-yoka, who had accompanied him, sat at a table. The council members dictated words to her. She had to set them down in Sequoyah's syllabary. If Ah-yoka could manage this challenge, the test would succeed.

Sequoyah's success depended on a ten-year-old girl. Could she write down what the council members dictated? Could she keep cool, or would she panic with so many stern eyes upon her? The council members were ready to condemn this crazy experiment, and Ah-yoka knew how much depended upon her.

Ah-yoka's ordeal was over at last. The door opened. Sequoyah entered the room. Ah-yoka sat quietly and gave no sign. The air was heavy with suspense. Sequoyah picked up the paper and saw that Ah-yoka had filled the paper with his symbols.

He was dizzy for a moment. Then he straightened up and began to read. He read aloud every word the council members had dictated. The talking leaves had spoken— in Cherokee!

The council members were amazed. Then the silence broke, and noisy excitement filled the room. The Cherokee nation had a written language.

The next years were miraculous. The Cherokees learned to read and write in a shorter time than any other group had anywhere. Eastern and Western Cherokees sent letters back and forth. Within a year the Cherokee nation had risen from illiteracy to a high degree of *literacy*.

What had Sequoyah accomplished? As C. Fayne Porter says, "He had done something which no man before him had done and which no man following him has done—he is the only person in the entire history of the world to invent, completely by himself, a simple and practicable alphabet or syllabary. It was a beautifully uncomplicated tool, capable of expressing the complete language and thought of the Cherokees. It was unquestionably the work of pure genius."

In the Cherokee nation, magazines and newspapers appeared. Schools sprang up. Sequoyah was a hero. He became one of the head men of the Western Nation. His name became famous outside the Cherokee nation. Other Americans admired his achievement. In 1847 the sequoia tree was named for him.

Filled with honors and years, Sequoyah could have rested on his laurels, but he kept searching. He thought he could find a key to link all Indian languages together. In 1842, when he was in his seventies, he set out with a small party of explorers. He traveled through the Southwest and Mexico. He talked with other Indians and kept searching for the common key.

He never found it. Sometime in 1843, Sequoyah died, but his work lived on. In 1980 the United States Post Office issued a stamp in his honor.

UNDERSTANDING WHAT YOU HAVE READ

Finding Another Title

1. Another good title for this selection might be (a) The Importance of Language (b) Ah-yoka: Heroine of the Cherokee (c) How the Cherokees Got a Written Language (d) The Development of Spoken Language.

Getting the Main Idea

2. Which of the following best states the main idea of the selection?
   (a) The written language goes back about 8,000 years.
   (b) Sequoyah had to overcome many difficulties to create the Cherokee written language.
   (c) Sequoyah's fellow Cherokees had faith in him from the beginning.
   (d) Sequoyah had to go west to succeed in his life's work.

Finding Details

3. All the following are mentioned as writing materials EXCEPT (a) clay (b) tree bark (c) papyrus (d) oak leaf.
4. Sequoyah's home and garden were neglected because he (a) became interested in picture writing (b) enlisted in the U.S. Army (c) lost his job on a plantation (d) lost interest in life.
5. The object that Ah-yoka found was (a) a bracelet (b) a pen (c) an envelope (d) a book.
6. A language that uses picture writing is (a) Cherokee (b) English (c) Chinese (d) German.

7. To get to the Mississippi River, Sequoyah traveled through (a) the Allegheny Mountains (b) the western desert (c) parts of Florida (d) the Great Smoky Mountains.
8. In its final form, the Cherokee written language had (a) 26 letters (b) 86 symbols (c) 200 symbols (d) thousands of symbols.
9. At the time of her great language challenge, Ahyoka was (a) six years old (b) living with her mother (c) ten years old (d) already married.
10. Sequoyah's written language was accepted and used by the Cherokee (a) within a year (b) very slowly (c) by 1812 (d) in the East but not the West.

Making Inferences

11. Sequoyah first got the idea for his project from (a) his experiences in the Army (b) a wise counselor of the Cherokee (c) his kind wife (d) watching his daughter play in the sand.
12. Sequoyah's achievement is especially remarkable because when he started, he (a) was ten years old (b) couldn't read or write (c) had only a speaking knowledge of English (d) worried that he would fail.
13. Sequoyah lost his friends because they (a) thought he was strange (b) didn't like his housekeeping (c) disliked his wife (d) felt the sting of his sharp tongue.
14. A written language that matches sounds and words (a) is called picture writing (b) can work with few letters or syllables (c) is rare (d) is found even among tribal societies.

15. The Cherokees quickly adopted Sequoyah's written language because they **(a)** felt sorry for him **(b)** wanted to read two languages: English and Cherokee **(c)** needed such a language badly **(d)** could set the language on tree bark.

Predicting What Happens Next

16. After the death of Sequoyah, **(a)** the syllabary died with him **(b)** his first wife took up the cause **(c)** he was soon forgotten **(d)** his written language continued to be used.

Deciding on the Order of Events

17. The following events are scrambled. Arrange them in proper order, as they happened. Use letters only.
    (a) Sequoyah travels to Mexico.
    (b) Sequoyah joins the U.S. Army.
    (c) Sequoyah's language passes the test in the Cherokee council.
    (d) Sequoyah becomes a stepfather.

Inferring Attitude

18. The attitude of C. Fayne Porter (90) toward the development of a written language is one of **(a)** respect for the difficulty **(b)** irritation at the delays **(c)** amusement at the challenge **(d)** impatience.

Separating Facts from Opinions

For each of the following, tell whether the statement is a fact (*F*) or an opinion (*O*).

19. Sequoyah's achievement is the greatest in the history of language.
20. Sequoyah developed the Cherokee written language.

Understanding Words from Context

21. Every group of people has a spoken language; it is *universal*.
    Universal (89) means (a) unusually large (b) widely talked about (c) present everywhere (d) tried and true.
22. None of these languages were simple. Even in tribal societies the language spoken was *complex*.
    Complex (89) means (a) colorful (b) easy (c) complicated (d) interesting.
23. Porter asked, "How many thousands of years did it take to produce and *refine* the alphabet with which this page is written?"
    Refine (90) means (a) discover (b) invent (c) explore (d) polish.
24. Scorned and *humiliated,* he left home with his six-year-old daughter, Ah-yoka.
    Humiliated (91) means (a) dishonored (b) physically injured (c) scolded (d) annoyed.
25. Within a year the Cherokee nation, which had not been able to read or write, had risen to a high degree of *literacy*.
    Literacy (94) means *the ability to* (a) speak and listen (b) read and write (c) invent and discover (d) think and consider.

THINKING IT OVER

1. How did Sequoyah show unusual strength of character in his struggle to create a Cherokee written language?
2. How important was the role played by Ah-yoka? Explain.
3. For some people watching television has replaced reading. Can television and the spoken language make the written language unnecessary? Explain.
4. Why did the Indians refer to books as "talking leaves"?
5. Why is an alphabet more convenient than picture writing?
6. Picture writing plays a role in our lives. Think of traffic signs, signs for bicyclists, directional signals. Why is such picture writing especially important when one is traveling in foreign countries?

ANOTHER LOOK AT THE QUOTATION

The grand essentials to happiness in this life are something to do, something to love, and something to hope for.
JOSEPH ADDISON

1. Explain the quotation in your own words.
2. Apply the quotation to Sequoyah's life. What was the "something to do"? Who or what was the "something to love"? What was the "something to hope for"? Was Sequoyah happy? Explain your answer.
3. Someone said we are happiest when we do not think about ourselves. Do you agree? Why or why not?

WORDS AT YOUR SERVICE—PARADOX

Because Sequoyah was not worldly-wise, he was free.
(90)
    Yet this misfortune turned out to be lucky. (91)

How can lack of worldly wisdom bring freedom? How can misfortune be lucky? Life is filled with contradictions, opposite ideas that exist together. It *is* true that misfortune sometimes has fortunate results, as it did for Sequoyah. When we state this situation in language, we call it a *paradox*. Sequoyah's life contains another paradox. When his wife destroyed his picture writing, she actually did him a favor. How did this cruel deed have good results?

Sometimes statements are paradoxical. Why is the following statement a paradox?

I never say *never*.

Work together with a group of students. Brainstorm to list as many paradoxes as you can.

JOE MONTANA:
"The Comeback Kid"

*Difficulties, opposition, criticism—these
things are meant to be overcome, and
there is a special joy in facing them and
in coming out on top.*
VIJAYA LAKSHMI PANDIT

The 1985 Super Bowl in the National Football League had one of the best matchups in history. The San Francisco Forty-Niners were playing the Miami Dolphins. Both teams had had outstanding records in the regular season. Both teams had sparkled in the playoff games leading up to Super Bowl 19. Even more important, the game matched two of the best quarterbacks against each other.

Dan Marino of Miami was a young player. This was only his second year in professional football. But he had made a record number of touchdown passes. In game after game, he had found his receivers and destroyed the opposition. It seemed impossible to stop him.

Joe Montana of San Francisco was a little older than Dan. He had had six years of experience in the professional ranks. Like Dan, he had played extremely well during the season and had led his team to victory in game after game.

"Will the amazing young Marino be able to outplay the more experienced Montana? Will the Forty-Niner defense be able to keep Marino from the goal line?" For weeks the arguments raged back and forth. Each team had its fans. Each group of fans was sure its own quarterback would *prevail* and its own team would win the game.

In January 1985, the big day arrived. The Dolphins started strong. The first time they got the ball, they scored a field goal. The next time they got it, they scored a touchdown. Miami quickly led, 10–7.

The Miami fans were looking forward to a great day. But then things changed. The Forty-Niners got stronger. They put pressure on Marino. Four times they tackled him before he could throw the ball. Miami's running game was already weak, and its passing became less effective.

Joe Montana started to control the game. His leadership of the team became more and more apparent. His runners made long gains. His passes found their targets.

When in trouble, he scrambled and ran. He scored a touchdown himself. When the game ended, the Forty-Niners had won, 38–16.

The Forty-Niners had many heroes. Roger Craig and Wendell Tyler had run powerfully and effectively. Dan Johnson, Fred Dean, and Dwaine Board had played strong defensive games. But at the center of the Forty-Niners' success was the team's great quarterback, Joe Montana.

Montana's opponents praised his ability. Miami guard Bob Baumhower said, "It was like chasing a rabbit out there."

Montana's rival, Dan Marino, admitted, "I didn't play as well as I could have. Sometimes I had a chance to move, and I didn't. It's necessary for a quarterback, and it's what Montana did so well today."

Montana later said, "As far as my own game, well, I'd have to admit it was pretty close to the best I've ever played. I didn't throw anything I didn't have confidence in. We got in sort of a groove. Once you get going like that you gain confidence, and it carries over to the defense, and then back to the offense. It's a snowball kind of thing."

Joe was too modest. Winning games is his trademark. His entire career has been a success story.

Joe was born on June 11, 1956, in Monongahela, Pennsylvania. He is of Italian descent, but one of his ancestors was a Sioux Indian. As a boy, Joe dreamed of becoming a great athlete like Joe Namath, another Pennsylvanian.

Joe's father was intensely interested in sports. When Joe was only eight months old, his father gave him a baseball and bat! His father put up a basketball hoop in the backyard. He put up a tire for Joe to throw footballs through. As a result, Joe *excelled* in many sports.

Joe was an all-around star athlete in high school and was sure to get an athletic scholarship to college. He was all set to go to North Carolina State University as a basketball player. Then Notre Dame University came through with a football scholarship.

At Notre Dame, Joe pulled off many miracles and even had a song created for him: "The Ballad of Joe Montana." He got the name the "Comeback Kid."

The first of Joe's many miracle comebacks was at North Carolina in 1975. In the last quarter of the football game, North Carolina was winning, 14–6. Within one minute and two seconds Joe passed Notre Dame to victory and a 21–14 score.

His second miracle comeback came against the Air Force Academy. In the second half the Air Force had piled up an almost impossible lead, 30–10. Joe Montana entered the game. In eight minutes he threw three touchdown passes to win the game, 31–30.

The next year, 1976, looked promising for Joe, but he was soon unhappy, not *optimistic*. A shoulder separation kept him from playing. He sat out the season and wondered if his career might be over.

At the beginning of 1977, he was only the third-string quarterback sitting on the bench. In the third game of the season, he was put into the game after the quarterback on the field was injured. When Joe went in, Purdue was leading, 24–10. Once again Joe pulled off a miracle. He completed nine of 14 passes and scored three touchdowns. Notre Dame won, 31–24.

This achievement made him the starting quarterback for the rest of the season. It was a great season. At the end of it, Notre Dame was ranked fifth and earned a chance to play in the Cotton Bowl, on January 2, 1978. The opponent was powerful Texas.

Texas came to the Cotton Bowl ranked first. The team had been undefeated in the regular season and was favored to beat Notre Dame. Joe's team turned the tables in a game that was a lot like the 1985 Super Bowl. Notre

Dame defeated Texas, 38–10, and won a first-place ranking.

Montana hadn't used up all the items in his bag of tricks. In the 1978 season, Pittsburgh was leading, 17–7, with only eight minutes left. To win, Notre Dame had to score two touchdowns and hold Pittsburgh scoreless. Every football fan knows that job isn't easy against a team like Pittsburgh. Joe Montana came from behind again. He completed 15 of 25 passes and won the game, 26–17.

One of the wildest games in history was perhaps Joe's happiest and saddest. Late in the 1978 season, the University of Southern California was leading Notre Dame. The score was 24–6, with 42 seconds left. Joe turned the score around to 27–25 in favor of Notre Dame. But then USC won the game with a last-second field goal.

In January 1979, Joe played his last college game. It was the Cotton Bowl, Notre Dame against Houston. Joe, too ill to play, was *ailing* and on the sidelines through most of the game. Late in the third quarter, Houston was leading, 34–12. Joe was weak, but he asked to get into the game. He completed pass after pass, touchdown after touchdown. He won the game, 35–34. The final touchdown came with only seconds to play.

Then came a surprise. Joe's college record was almost unbelievably good, but many professional scouts were *dubious* about him. They were uncertain about the long-term strength and accuracy of his passing arm. Professional teams take turns choosing football players. This method, called the *draft,* gives everyone a chance to get good players.

The very best players are chosen on the first round. Exceptional players are chosen on the second round. Surely Joe was exceptional, but no team chose him on either round.

Bill Walsh, coach of the San Francisco Forty-Niners,

had his eye on Montana, though. Walsh felt that the scouts did not realize just how good Montana was. Walsh needed the players he chose on the first two rounds. But when the third round came along, Walsh quickly selected Montana.

When asked why he chose Montana, Walsh replied, "People who say his is only an average arm are mistaken. And they always will be. Because his delivery is not a flick of the wrist like Terry Bradshaw's, they think it's not strong. He throws on the run while avoiding a pass rush, and he does not have to be totally set. He is not a moving platform like some others, who are mechanical and can only do well when everything is just right. Joe performs just as well under stress."

Some credit for Joe's success must be given to coach Walsh. Sometimes new players are put into action too soon. They do poorly and become *disheartened*. Walsh worked Montana into the lineup gradually. He paired Joe with another new player, receiver Dwight Clark. They developed a good relationship. Dwight seemed to know just where Joe would throw the ball. Joe believed that Dwight could catch a ball that was anywhere near him. That partnership paid off later in 1982 in a playoff game against Dallas. Joe and Dwight made one of the great plays of football.

Steve DeBerg was the starting quarterback for the Forty-Niners in 1979. Joe had to wait his turn. When DeBerg was traded, Joe came into his own.

On December 7, 1980, the Forty-Niners played the New Orleans Saints. At halftime the Saints were ahead by 28 points. Rarely does any team overcome such a handicap. Joe's efforts at this point reminded fans of the Notre Dame games. He led the team in four touchdown drives to tie the score. Then in overtime he brought the team down for a field goal to win the game, 38–35.

The 1980 team record, however, was not good. The Forty-Niners won six games and lost ten. Joe resolved that 1981 would be different. It was.

In 1981 the team won 13 games to gain a spot in the playoffs. On January 10, 1982, the Forty-Niners played the Dallas Cowboys. The Cowboys were favored to win, but the Forty-Niners had Joe Montana.

Late in the game Dallas was leading. Then Joe threw a high pass to the outstretched arms of his old partner, Dwight Clark. Clark made a miraculous catch, and the Forty-Niners went on to win, 28–27.

This victory led to Joe's first Super Bowl, on January 24, 1982, against the Cincinnati Bengals. Montana himself scored the first touchdown and passed for others. The Forty-Niners won, 26–21.

The 1982 season was shortened by a players' strike, and the Forty-Niners did not do well. But they could not be kept down forever. As we have seen, the Forty-Niners had a successful 1984 season and a magnificent Super Bowl.

You may recall that Bill Walsh said, "Joe performs just as well under stress." That last sentence lifts Joe Montana above most of his rivals. Joe is excellent under pressure. He is a leader who takes responsibility for his team. He inspires confidence. His players believe that Joe can lead them through difficulties. He can be perfectly calm while three giant linemen are bearing down on him. He can get the ball away, although he knows he'll be tackled hard a split second later.

Joe pays attention to details, and he keeps his eye on the important things as well. He is basically calm, pleasant, and good-humored. He spends much time studying the game, but his concentration doesn't make him nervous. He is calm with his players. He can get emotional in tense moments, but he never loses his temper.

He doesn't particularly look like a football player. He has blue eyes, blond hair, and a boyish smile. He has a relaxed personality, but when the Forty-Niners have the ball, watch out! Players on opposing teams have learned to respect this easygoing, gentle person.

UNDERSTANDING WHAT YOU HAVE READ

Finding Another Title

1. Another good title for this selection might be **(a)** The 1985 Super Bowl **(b)** One of Football's Great Team Leaders **(c)** The College Career of Joe Montana **(d)** How to Win at Football.

Getting the Main Idea

2. Joe's major strength as a player is **(a)** his refusal to give up **(b)** a gentle personality **(c)** the most powerful arm in football **(d)** luck.

Finding Details

3. The Forty-Niners won Super Bowl 19 by a score of **(a)** 31–24 **(b)** 38–10 **(c)** 26–17 **(d)** 38–16.
4. Two members of the Forty-Niner football team are **(a)** Roger Craig and Wendell Tyler **(b)** Bob Baumhower and Dwaine Board **(c)** Terry Bradshaw and Dan Johnson **(d)** Fred Dean and Joe Namath.
5. The year of Joe Montana's birth is **(a)** 1954 **(b)** 1956 **(c)** 1957 **(d)** not mentioned.

6. At first, Joe was planning to play basketball at **(a)** Purdue **(b)** Pittsburgh **(c)** Houston **(d)** North Carolina State University.
7. Notre Dame won a first-place ranking by defeating **(a)** the University of Southern California **(b)** Miami **(c)** Texas **(d)** Houston.
8. Though he was ill, Joe came into a game against **(a)** Penn State **(b)** Houston **(c)** Texas **(d)** Dallas.
9. In the football draft, Joe Montana was chosen **(a)** on the first round **(b)** on the second round **(c)** on the third round **(d)** on the fourth round.
10. All the following are mentioned as college opponents of Notre Dame EXCEPT **(a)** Purdue **(b)** Air Force Academy **(c)** Pittsburgh **(d)** New Orleans.

Making Inferences

11. The Super Bowl 19 score can best be described as **(a)** fair **(b)** unfair **(c)** surprising **(d)** sad.
12. Joe owes a great deal of his interest in sports to **(a)** his coach at Notre Dame **(b)** Dan Marino **(c)** his father **(d)** Dwight Clark.
13. Notre Dame was most likely ranked first after the 1978 Cotton Bowl because **(a)** it had defeated Purdue earlier in the season **(b)** it had defeated first-ranked Texas **(c)** the Notre Dame coaches had special influence with sportswriters **(d)** Joe Montana had come back after a shoulder separation.
14. Coach Walsh's handling of Joe Montana's career can be called **(a)** one-sided **(b)** lucky **(c)** hasty **(d)** wise.
15. Winning a football game depends most on **(a)** teamwork **(b)** superior speed **(c)** guesswork **(d)** strict quarterbacks.

Predicting What Happens Next

16. When Joe Montana was interviewed months after
the Super Bowl victory, he most likely   **(a)** shouted,
"We did it!"   **(b)** spoke with calm satisfaction
(c) boasted about beating Marino   **(d)** took major
credit for winning.

Deciding on the Order of Events

17. The following events are scrambled. Arrange them
in proper order, as they happened. Use letters only.
(a)   Joe accepts a football scholarship to Notre Dame.
(b)   The Forty-Niners defeat the Dolphins in the
Super Bowl.
(c)   Joe scores late in the game to defeat the University of Southern California.
(d)   The Forty-Niners defeat the Bengals in the Super
Bowl.

Inferring Tone

18. Bill Walsh's description of Joe Montana's abilities
(106) is   **(a)** realistic and appreciative   **(b)** enthusiastic but worried   **(c)** humorous and lighthearted   **(d)** slightly approving.

Separating Facts from Opinions

For each of the following, tell whether the statement
is a fact (*F*) or an opinion (*O*).
19. Joe Montana came from behind to win against New
Orleans.
20. Bill Walsh is probably the most skillful coach in
professional football.

Understanding Words from Context

21. Each group of fans was sure its own quarterback would *prevail* and its team would win the game.
    Prevail (102) means **(a)** win out **(b)** miss passes **(c)** run the football **(d)** play the full game.
22. Although Joe played football well, he *excelled* in many other sports.
    Excelled (103) means **(a)** played occasionally **(b)** was exceptionally good **(c)** took an active part in **(d)** found many competitors.
23. Joe, too ill to play, was *ailing* on the sidelines through most of the game.
    Ailing (105) means **(a)** sitting **(b)** observing **(c)** sick **(d)** alert.
24. Joe's college record was almost unbelievably good, but many professional scouts were *dubious* about him.
    Dubious (105) means **(a)** excited **(b)** uninterested **(c)** fearful **(d)** doubtful.
25. They do poorly and become *disheartened*.
    Disheartened (106) means **(a)** weary **(b)** angry **(c)** noisy **(d)** discouraged.

THINKING IT OVER

1. How did Joe Montana show qualities of good leadership on the field?
2. Athletes are given college scholarships to play various sports. Some people think these athletes should also be paid, since their efforts bring in a great deal of money to the colleges. What do you think?
3. Does watching sports on television make young people

less athletic, or does it encourage them to get out and exercise more? Explain.

4. In a number of polls, football has been named the most popular sport on television. Why is it more popular than basketball, hockey, soccer, or baseball?
5. The Super Bowl is one of the biggest of all television attractions, but many people consider the promotion and advertising overdone. Do you agree? Why or why not?

ANOTHER LOOK AT THE QUOTATION

> *Difficulties, opposition, criticism—these things are meant to be overcome, and there is a special joy in facing them and coming out on top.*
> VIJAYA LAKSHMI PANDIT

1. Explain the quotation in your own words.
2. How did Joe Montana demonstrate the truth of this quotation?
3. When you play competitive sports, do you usually play better when you are losing or winning? How do you feel when you come out on top? Explain.

WORDS AT YOUR SERVICE—ANTONYMS

The next year, 1976, looked promising for Joe, but he was soon unhappy, not *optimistic.* (104)

On page 54 we explained how two paired words can help

you find the meaning of one word in the pair. These words are synonyms. Sometimes words are paired with *not* in between. Notice that *unhappy* and *optimistic* are paired in the sentence above. But this time the word *not* tells you that these words are opposites. Words that are opposite are called *antonyms.* *Unhappy* and *optimistic* are antonyms. The word *not* tells you that *optimistic* is an antonym of *unhappy.* To make the meaning clearer, a writer sometimes provides antonyms in the same sentence. One of the antonyms is usually easier than the other. This helps you understand the less familiar word.

Study the following sentences and then guess the meaning of each *italicized* word. Use the antonyms to help you.

EXAMPLE

Jody was a rock star, but when he was offstage, his clothes were ordinary, not *offbeat.*
Offbeat means **(a)** worn **(b)** colorless **(c)** unattractive **(d)** unusual.
Offbeat is clearly the opposite of *ordinary.* The correct answer is **(d)** *unusual.*

1. The bank account began to *dwindle,* not increase.
   Dwindle means **(a)** grow **(b)** draw more interest **(c)** get less and less **(d)** become a burden.
2. The audience expected Hanson to praise the candidate, not *denounce* him.
   Denounce means **(a)** criticize **(b)** announce **(c)** talk about **(d)** nominate.
3. After the accident the clock in the auto was still *intact,* not broken.
   Intact means **(a)** smashed **(b)** out of order **(c)** highly polished **(d)** undamaged.
4. After I had won the lawsuit, my friends expected to find me happy, not *forlorn.*

Forlorn means (a) bright and cheerful (b) sad and lonely (c) dull and uninteresting (d) quiet and unfriendly.

5. Jerry is too slender, not *stocky* enough to play guard on our school football team.
Stocky means (a) light on one's feet (b) tall (c) solidly built (d) flabby.

COMPLETING AN OUTLINE

The article on Joe Montana might be outlined in the following way. Five outline items have been omitted. Test your understanding of the structure of the article by following the directions after the outline.

I. Super Bowl 19
   A. Outstanding matchup of teams
   B.
   C. San Francisco victory
   D. Montana's role

II. Early years
   A. Birth in Monongahela, Pennsylvania
   B. Father's interest in sports
   C.

III. The college years
   A.
   B. Fame for breathtaking comebacks
   C. Year of disappointment—1976
   D. Victory in Cotton Bowl
   E. Later victories

IV. Professional career
   A.
   B. Gradual development as professional
   C. Improvement of team's performance
   D. Super Bowl against Cincinnati
   E. Super Bowl against Miami

V. Personality
   A. Leadership abilities
   B. Skill under pressure
   C.
   D. Understanding of the game

Fill in the items omitted from the outline. Correctly match the items in column A with the outline numbers in column B, which show where each item belongs in the outline.

A		B	
1.	Scholarship to Notre Dame	a.	I. B.
2.	Relaxed manner	b.	II. C.
3.	Battle of leading quarterbacks	c.	III. A.
4.	Choice on third round in draft	d.	IV. A
5.	Excellence in high school sports	e.	V. C.

ANOTHER LOOK

HOW MUCH DO YOU REMEMBER?

1. The two who were interested in the problems of the cities are (a) Sequoyah and Henry Cisneros (b) Joe Montana and Patricia Roberts Harris (c) Sequoyah and Patricia Roberts Harris (d) Henry Cisneros and Patricia Roberts Harris.
2. Sequoyah (a) explored the Far West (b) helped create a written language (c) was the highest chief of the Cherokees (d) died in Washington, D.C.
3. Joe Montana (a) once ran for Congress (b) was a friend of Henry Cisneros (c) often came from behind to win (d) played football at San Antonio.
4. The person once considered as a candidate for vice president of the United States is (a) Patricia Roberts Harris (b) Henry Cisneros (c) Daniel Patrick Moynihan (d) none of these.
5. The "Talking Leaves" are (a) pages with writing (b) television scripts (c) video cassettes (d) young actors.
6. Joe Montana played in the Super Bowls of 1982 and 1985 and (a) won both (b) won the first and lost the second (c) lost the first and won the second (d) lost both.

7. Henry Cisneros and Joe Montana are alike in that they **(a)** were born in Texas **(b)** believe in luck **(c)** were friends of Patricia Roberts Harris **(d)** are very popular leaders.
8. An important quality of Patricia Roberts Harris was **(a)** her ability to get her job done in eight hours **(b)** her use of favoritism to get results **(c)** her ability to learn from criticism **(d)** her unwillingness to forgive a wrong.
9. Widespread popular education is difficult without **(a)** telephones **(b)** a written language **(c)** teachers trained in Washington **(d)** films and video cassettes.
10. In his winning record, Joe Montana showed many examples of **(a)** leadership **(b)** impatience **(c)** lack of understanding **(d)** worry.

WHAT IS YOUR OPINION?

1. Which person in this unit seems to be the most effective leader? Explain.
2. Leaders differ. For example, Sequoyah was a quiet leader. Patricia Harris never took a back seat. What do you think are the most important qualities a good leader must have?
3. Is it easier to lead or to follow? Explain.
4. What qualities do Americans look for in the president they vote for? Which qualities *should* they look for?
5. Henry Cisneros and Patricia Harris are both associated with politics. Politics and politicians sometimes get a bad name. Why? Isn't politics the very heart of democracy?

THE QUOTATION AND THE UNIT

> *No amount of study or learning will*
> *make a man a leader unless he has the*
> *natural qualities of one.*
> SIR ARCHIBALD WAVELL

1. Explain the quotation in your own words.
2. Are there bad leaders as well as good leaders? How can you tell a bad leader?
3. Did the subjects in this unit have "the natural qualities" of leadership? Explain.
4. What does the quotation by Arnold Glasow on page 60 mean? "Candidates who straddle important issues are taken for a ride."
5. Have you noticed, in your own experience, that some of your classmates seem to be natural leaders? How can you spot a natural leader?

3

LIVING FOR ADVENTURE

My favorite thing is to go where I've never been.

DIANE ARBUS

Diane Arbus gives us a good definition of *adventure.* Most of us have a yearning at times to go where we've never been. The four subjects in this unit have all satisfied that yearning.

Paul Newman gets adventure by racing fast cars and testing his own skills. Each new race is a spot "where he's never been." Matthew Henson got his adventure by traveling to distant places. He went somewhere he'd

119

never been before. He also went where *no one* had ever gone before: the North Pole.

Sacajawea found adventure with the Lewis and Clark Expedition. She traveled through strange and unfamiliar lands and at last looked upon the great Pacific Ocean.

Sally Ride's adventure was truly "out of this world." As the first American woman to fly in space, she blazed a trail for others to follow.

Adventure is not only physical experience. There are adventures of the mind and spirit too. William Feather advises, "One way to get the most out of life is to look upon it as an adventure." Every moment is new. At every moment you are going where you've never been. Life itself is an adventure.

PAUL NEWMAN:
Superstar

*You're in for a great deal of pain if you
take yourself too seriously.*

PAUL NEWMAN

"**P**aul-o Newman! Paul-o Newman!"

The workers in the fields of Italy once caught a glimpse of Paul Newman walking by. They knew at once who he was. They shouted his name 'in honest admiration. Paul Newman cannot escape this instant identification. Wherever he goes, people know him. Italian peasants, English tradespeople, French taxi drivers—everyone knows Paul Newman.

There are hundreds of Hollywood stars, but only a few superstars. Paul Newman is a superstar.

Paul Newman never looked for such admiration. He is basically a modest man. He has a true understanding of his strengths and weaknesses. He cannot avoid his fame, but he doesn't let it change him.

Surprisingly, fame came late to Paul Newman. He was born in Cleveland Heights, Ohio, in 1925. He hadn't the slightest idea that he would become a professional actor some day. He acted in children's groups and school plays, but so did many others. If someone had said, "You'll become one of the most famous actors of your time," he would have laughed out loud.

Because he was small as a boy, he was often bullied by bigger boys. He took his troubles in stride and learned physical courage.

Paul enlisted in the Navy in 1942, but he failed the physical. His famous blue eyes turned out to be color-blind. He did, however, get into the Air Corps. He saw active duty in torpedo planes and in submarine patrols off Guam, Hawaii, and Saipan. But he didn't see serious combat. He was never wounded. In describing his war experiences, he said with his usual sense of humor, "I got through the whole war on two razor blades."

At Kenyon College in Ohio, Paul tried out for football. He was dropped from the second-string team. He joined the student dramatic society for something to do.

The drama professor was very much impressed with Paul's acting ability. Paul, however, thought himself a very bad actor. This self-criticism is typical of Paul. He thinks he doesn't have much natural talent for acting. He does think he can concentrate, though. Paul's fans would disagree with Paul's too-modest comments.

Paul graduated from Kenyon College in 1949 and spent a season in a summer playhouse. Then he moved to Woodstock, Illinois, and joined the Woodstock Players. He met an actress, Jacqueline Witte, and married her. They were divorced later.

Then came a shock. Paul's father died and Paul went back home. He gave up all ideas of serious acting and became a salesperson in his father's store.

Suppose Paul had stayed on as a salesperson? What might have happened? We'll never know. The family decided to sell the store, and Paul was on his own.

In September 1951, he took his wife, Jackie, and their son, Scott, and headed to New Haven. There he enrolled in the Yale University School of Drama.

Why did he go back to acting? Was there some sudden need to act? Did Paul feel a great drive to become a professional actor? Not at all. Paul says, "I wasn't driven to acting by any inner *compulsion.* I was running away from the sporting goods business."

Paul was then 26. This is an age when most professional actors and performers are established in their work. Paul was really just beginning. He had only $900 in the bank and needed to earn money.

Paul got some experience at Yale and then went to New York. His good looks got him a few small parts on television. Then he made $150 a week as an *understudy* to Ralph Meeker in *Picnic,* a play by William Inge.

While Meeker was on vacation, Paul took the leading role. On the strength of this experience he spoke to the director, Josh Logan. "Can I take Meeker's role when the play goes on the road?" he asked.

Logan refused. He claimed that Paul was not quite good enough. Things started to look up for Paul, though. He began to get serious about his job. He enrolled in the Actors Studio. Among his fellow students in the school were Geraldine Page and Rod Steiger.

The movies came next. Warner Brothers gave Paul a long-term movie contract. His starting salary was $1,000 a week. His first movie role was terrible! He played a Greek slave in a historical drama called *The Silver Chalice*. Paul considers this the worst picture ever made. It played on television in Los Angeles years later. When it did, Paul took out a large ad in the *Los Angeles Times:* "Paul Newman Apologizes Every Night This Week."

Paul learned a valuable lesson from this picture. Not every film will be a hit. Some films will be box office failures. Sometimes no one can be sure until a film actually faces an audience. Paul has had his share of hits and flops. But he's always ready to take a chance, both onscreen and offscreen.

There were many great pictures too. Many of them appear and reappear on television. Paul attracted other stars and worked with the most famous. In 1958 he appeared with Elizabeth Taylor in *Cat on a Hot Tin Roof.* In 1961 he made *The Hustler* with Jackie Gleason. In 1963 he made *Hud* with Patricia Neal. In 1966 he starred in *Harper* with Lauren Bacall.

One of Paul's favorites is *Cool Hand Luke.* It is the story of a brave *loner* on a prison chain gang, a man who looks only to himself for support and comfort. This film is considered a screen masterpiece. *Hombre,* which he also made in 1967, showed how fine a Western could be.

Movie after movie had the Newman touch and success at the box office. Then, in 1969, came a *blockbuster* of a movie, not just an average success. Someone had the brilliant idea of putting Robert Redford and Paul Newman in the same movie. The result was *Butch Cassidy and the Sundance Kid*. With great charm, the movie poked fun at Westerns. Redford and Newman played together as if they had been pals all their lives. The action was fast, furious, and funny.

How could Redford and Newman top *Butch Cassidy and the Sundance Kid*? In 1973 they appeared in *The Sting*. This movie has a good plot and excellent characters. It also has a musical background of great charm. It uses some of the lovely ragtime melodies of Scott Joplin. Joplin was a musical genius who died in 1917 almost unknown. *The Sting* brought his music back to great popularity.

Through all these movies, Paul worked with ease and relaxation. One of his screenwriters said of Paul, "He makes it look so easy, and he looks so wonderful, that everybody assumes he isn't acting."

Paul continued to make great movies. He didn't stick to one type of film but tried all kinds. He didn't have a need to make himself look glamorous. In *The Verdict* he played a beaten-down lawyer who drank too much. In *Slap Shot* he played a clumsy, unattractive, losing hockey coach. Paul has great courage.

The courage appears again and again in his private life.

Paul is an expert race-car driver. He likes to race in the summer season and make films at other times. He began racing in his late forties and became one of the best amateur drivers in the country. He has been national champion in his class twice and is respected by other drivers. He races hard and well. There is always danger driving at great speeds on crowded tracks. But Paul ignores this danger. To Paul, life is an adventure. He lives it to the full.

Paul lives many lives. He is a movie superstar and a skilled racing driver. He is also a successful businessman.

Paul thinks he makes the world's best salad dressing. Once, in an expensive restaurant, he washed a salad clean of all dressing and then made his own salad dressing at the table. He began to manufacture the dressing as *Newman's Own Olive Oil and Vinegar Dressing*. He became interested in marketing spaghetti sauce, too. He gives the profits to various good causes. One of the causes is the Scott Newman Foundation. This is an organization to combat the drug problem.

There is sadness in Paul's life too. In 1978 his son Scott, then 28, died of an overdose of painkillers and alcohol. The tragic death will never leave Paul. Some day he hopes to make a movie about his son's death.

Paul takes part in other causes. He has been active in the nuclear-freeze debate. In 1978 President Carter appointed him to a special session of the United Nations on disarmament.

His second marriage is a Hollywood success story. Paul married Joanne Woodward in the late 1950s. Joanne is a skilled actress, too, *ingenious* in bringing her roles to life. She is not a superstar like Paul, but she has many loyal fans.

Joanne and Paul are deeply attached to each other. They are quite different in personalities. But their differences cause no real problems. They understand each other and can laugh at their weaknesses. Their professional work sometimes separates them. Joanne doesn't object to Paul's racing, and Paul doesn't object to her different interests. As he once said, "We have a deal. I trade her a couple of ballets for a couple of races."

Joanne respects Paul's inner needs. She watches her husband race. She said, "Paul likes to test himself. That's what makes Paul run. He's got a lot of courage, a highly underrated element in people's lives these days."

Paul is a director as well as an actor. He likes to direct his wife in films. He says, "Given the right parts, she is a great actress. She can find so many different *facets* of herself to play. Those are two different people in *Rachel, Rachel* and *The Shadow Box*. That is magic."

The two occasionally act together in a movie. In *A New Kind of Love*, made in 1963, Joanne and Paul played together. Their fans enjoyed the movie. Paul says, "When we act together, we both know we can't get away with any old tricks, because the other one is sitting there nodding his head knowingly and saying, 'Yes, I seem to remember your doing that on the twenty-eighth page of *The Helen Morgan Story*.'"

Paul keeps himself in excellent physical shape. He runs three miles daily. His body is lean and muscular. He looks much younger than he is.

Paul is a rare actor who appeals to all groups. He appeals almost equally to men and women, to the young and the old. That sly smile and those bright blue eyes have helped make him a superstar. But there is a deeper quality to Paul. It shows in his acting.

UNDERSTANDING WHAT YOU HAVE READ

Finding Another Title

1. Another good title for this selection might be **(a)** How to Become a Star **(b)** From Rags to Riches **(c)** The Development of a Colorful Personality **(d)** Paul Newman: Race-Car Driver.

Getting the Main Idea

2. Paul Newman **(a)** has many interests and special abilities **(b)** once worked as a salesperson **(c)** is happily married to Joanne Woodward **(d)** has had a successful film every time.

Finding Details

3. During the Second World War Paul served in **(a)** the Army **(b)** the Navy **(c)** the Coast Guard **(d)** the Air Corps.
4. Kenyon College is in **(a)** Connecticut **(b)** Ohio **(c)** New York **(d)** California.
5. The Woodstock Players were in **(a)** New York **(b)** Ohio **(c)** Connecticut **(d)** Illinois.
6. Jacqueline Witte was **(a)** the female lead in *Cool Hand Luke* **(b)** Paul's first wife **(c)** the wife of Scott Newman **(d)** a classmate in Kenyon College.
7. Paul and his family went to New Haven in **(a)** 1925 **(b)** 1942 **(c)** 1951 **(d)** 1958.
8. A movie that poked fun at Westerns is **(a)** *Picnic* **(b)** *Butch Cassidy and the Sundance Kid* **(c)** *Harper* **(d)** *The Hustler*.

9. Scott Joplin was (a) a composer of ragtime music (b) the director of Paul Newman's first film (c) the owner of Paul Newman's racing car (d) an actor in the movie *Hombre*.

10. The two movies starring Redford and Newman were (a) *The Sting* and *The Verdict* (b) *Hud* and *Butch Cassidy and the Sundance Kid* (c) *The Sting* and *The Silver Chalice* (d) *Butch Cassidy and the Sundance Kid* and *The Sting*.

Making Inferences

11. Paul decided to return to Ohio after the death of his father. This decision showed Paul's (a) foolishness (b) acting ability (c) family loyalty (d) weakness.

12. It is reasonable to assume that the Actors Studio (a) helped many actors become successful (b) was connected with Yale University (c) was run by Robert Redford (d) was unpopular with Paul.

13. Paul Newman became famous throughout the world because of his (a) acting ability (b) salad dressing (c) race-car driving (d) marriage.

14. Which of the following statements can reasonably be made about Paul Newman and Joanne Woodward? (a) They understand and accept each other's faults. (b) They never disagree. (c) They have never made a movie together. (d) Each is envious of the other.

15. All the following statements may reasonably be made about Paul Newman EXCEPT (a) he enjoys working (b) he likes to try new things (c) he is afraid of failure (d) he is a good husband.

Predicting What Happens Next

16. After making *The Verdict,* Paul Newman probably (a) refused to act in Westerns (b) directed his
wife in the next three pictures (c) continued to look
for interesting scripts (d) tried to find parts that
made him look younger.

Deciding on the Order of Events

17. The following events are scrambled. Arrange them
in proper order, as they happened. Use letters only.
(a) Paul's father dies.
(b) Paul marries for the first time.
(c) *The Sting* is a great success.
(d) Paul Newman and Robert Redford act together
for the first time.

Inferring Tone

18. When Paul says (126) about Joanne, "We have a
deal," he is speaking (a) angrily (b) suspiciously
(c) affectionately (d) loudly.

Separating Facts from Opinions

For each of the following, tell whether the statement is
a fact (*F*) or an opinion (*O*).
19. Paul Newman has put out his own brand of salad
dressing.
20. Joanne Woodward has appeared with Paul in
movies.

Understanding Words from Context

21. Paul says, "I wasn't driven to acting by any inner
    compulsion."
    Compulsion (123) means **(a)** dislike **(b)** driving
    force **(c)** unhappiness **(d)** weariness.
22. Then he made $150 a week as an *understudy* to Ralph
    Meeker in *Picnic.*
    Understudy (123) means **(a)** substitute **(b)**
    enemy **(c)** fellow student **(d)** announcer.
23. *Cool Hand Luke* is the story of a brave *loner* on a
    prison chain gang, a man who looks only to himself
    for support and confidence.
    A *loner* (124) is *a person who* **(a)** makes trouble
    (b) is a hero **(c)** obeys orders **(d)** stays apart
    from others.
24. Joanne is a skilled actress, too, *ingenious* in bringing
    her roles to life.
    Ingenious (126) means **(a)** young **(b)** clever
    (c) uncertain **(d)** eager.
25. "She can find so many different *facets* of herself to
    play."
    Facets (127) means **(a)** sides **(b)** copies **(c)**
    films **(d)** weaknesses.

THINKING IT OVER

1. Is it possible that Paul Newman's late start as a
   professional actor helped his career? Explain your point
   of view.
2. Most successful people work hard to gain their success. Name two people who did well after much hard
   work. Tell what you know about them.
3. If Paul Newman is a superstar, who else in Hollywood
   is a superstar? Why did you choose him or her?

4. Paul has starred in a number of Westerns. Among them are *The Outrage, The Life and Times of Judge Roy Bean, Butch Cassidy and the Sundance Kid, Hud,* and *Hombre.* Have you ever seen one of these films? Tell about it. Do you enjoy Westerns? If so, what kind of Westerns do you like most?
5. Does Paul live for adventure? Explain.
6. Does being a celebrity create problems? Explain.
7. Paul and Joanne laugh a lot together. How does laughter help a marriage or a friendship?

ANOTHER LOOK AT THE QUOTATION

> *You're in for a great deal of pain if you take yourself too seriously.*
>
> PAUL NEWMAN

1. How is it possible for people to take themselves too seriously? Give examples.
2. How does taking yourself lightly help when trouble strikes?
3. How does Paul show in his life that he believes what he said?

WORDS AT YOUR SERVICE—CONTRAST

Then, in 1969, came a *blockbuster* of a movie, not just an average success. (125)

In earlier chapters you have studied how context can help you learn word meanings. Sometimes the whole sentence gives a clue. Sometimes words are paired, helping you decide the meaning of the unfamiliar word.

Another clue is contrast. *Contrast* means *difference*. Notice how the sentence above contains a contrast.

Though *success* and *blockbuster* are not antonyms (112), they are contrasted. The wording tells us that *blockbuster* is much more than an *average success*. It is a *huge success*.

Many words are used to express contrast. Some of these words are *not, but, although, though, never, instead, either–or, on the other hand*. These words and others like them can be very helpful in deciding a new word's meaning.

Study the following sentences and then guess the meaning of each *italicized* word. Call on contrast to help you.

EXAMPLE

Although Mark seemed to be *attentive,* he was actually daydreaming.

Attentive means **(a)** angry **(b)** observant **(c)** nervous **(d)** bold.

Attentive is contrasted with *daydreaming*. A person who is daydreaming will not be observant. The correct answer is **(b)** *observant*.

1. We expected Jerry to be *obstinate*. Instead he gave in right away.
   Obstinate means **(a)** gracious **(b)** careless **(c)** friendly **(d)** stubborn.
2. Marylu never shows signs of *frailty*. She is strong in dealing with her problems.
   Frailty means **(a)** strength **(b)** weakness **(c)** humor **(d)** sadness.
3. Dan wanted things his own way, but we finally *compromised*.
   Compromised means **(a)** completely disagreed **(b)** dropped the matter **(c)** each gave in a little **(d)** argued without a solution.

4. Although the clouds were *forbidding* all afternoon, they disappeared without developing into a storm. *Forbidding* means **(a)** disagreeing **(b)** sailing along **(c)** raiding **(d)** threatening.
5. Either *execute* the new plan, or drop it altogether. *Execute* means **(a)** condemn **(b)** change in small ways **(c)** put into effect **(d)** put up for a vote.

COMPLETING AN OUTLINE

The article on Paul Newman might be outlined in the following way. Five outline items have been omitted. Test your understanding of the structure of the article by following the directions after the outline.

   I. Early years
     A. Birth in Cleveland Heights
     B. Early acting experiences
     C. Service in Air Corps
     D.

  II. Turning points
     A. Death of his father
     B. Job in store
     C.
     D. Departure for Yale University

 III. First professional work
     A.
     B. Enrollment in Actors Studio
     C. Part in *The Silver Chalice*

IV. Success in the movies
A. Hits of the 1950s and 1960s
B. Paul's favorite: *Cool Hand Luke*
C.
D. Redford and Newman together again: *The Sting*
E. Later movies

V. Offscreen life
A.
B. Development of commercial products
C. Delegate to United Nations
D. Marriage to Joanne Woodward

Fill in the items omitted from the outline. Correctly match the items in column A with the outline numbers in column B, which show where each item belongs in the outline.

A	B
1. Major success: *Butch Cassidy and the Sundance Kid*	a. I. D.
	b. II. C.
	c. III. A.
2. Sale of store	d. IV. C.
3. Acting experience in Kenyon College	e. V. A.
4. Skill as racing driver	
5. Understudy in *Picnic*	

MATTHEW HENSON:
Arctic Explorer

*What is it that pulls me away from what
others call happiness, home and loved
ones; why does my love for them not
hold me down, root me? Games.
Adventures. The unknown.*

ANAÏS NIN

The moon and Mars and the other planets are places of mystery. Though the United States put men on the moon for a short time, this dead world is still mostly unexplored. Unmanned space ships have set down on Mars and sent back pictures of another place with many secrets. Still other spacecraft have gone past Saturn and Jupiter. Pictures from these space flights stir the imagination and *entice* us to further exploration. Who knows when the first human will set foot on Mars or on the worlds beyond?

A hundred years ago the North and South Poles were also places of mystery. Many explorers gave their lives trying to reach these forbidding lands. Yet as long as a challenge *persists,* men and women will keep trying.

The history of polar exploration is long. As far back as 325 B.C., a Greek mariner named Pytheas may have reached the Arctic Circle. In A.D. 484, an Irish monk, St. Brendan, described a "floating crystal castle." This may be the first mention of an iceberg in literature. Some people believe that St. Brendan reached the Arctic Circle.

In about A.D. 870, a Norse sailor named Ottar sailed around the North Cape of Norway and entered true polar waters. For nearly 500 years after that, the Norse sailed these northern waters. First they settled Iceland. Then Eric the Red explored the west. He set up Norse colonies on Greenland. Though these settlements lasted for nearly 500 years, they disappeared suddenly and mysteriously. Some experts believe that changes in climate were responsible for their disappearance.

The northern waters became especially important when explorers tried to find a direct route from Europe to China. They believed that a Northwest Passage would enable them to sail around the North American continent. Their efforts were doomed to failure. But the *quest* increased interest in the Arctic.

In 1844 Sir John Franklin set out on the newest, strongest ships of that time. The two ships, the *Erebus* and the *Terror,* had many clever features. For example, their propellers could be lifted clear of the ice, if necessary. Unfortunately, all those features could not save the ships.

The ships were trapped in crushing ice. During the second winter, Sir John died of illness. After the third winter his crew *perished* on a trip across the ice made in the hope of reaching safety. Of the 129 members of this expedition, not a single person survived. Forty expeditions took part in the hunt for Franklin and his companions. Though they did not find the explorers alive, they did add to the world's knowledge of the Arctic.

None of these expeditions ever came close to the North Pole. Still, many explorers yearned to be the first at the Pole. Lieutenant George Washington De Long set out in 1879. He hoped to drift with the pack ice and thus come close to the Pole. Soon after arriving at the pack ice, his ship, the *Jeannette,* was trapped. For 20 months the ship drifted barely 300 miles. For one brief moment in 1881, the water seemed to open up before the ship. De Long ordered full speed ahead. But the ice closed in and nearly crushed the ship.

The situation became desperate. De Long and his 32 companions set out across the ice. It was summer, the worst time for traveling across the ice. The snow was too soft for the sleds. The men slipped into pools of slush. Many of them fell sick, but they kept on.

They reached open water at last and set out in boats. One boat *capsized,* overturned by the sea. All in the boat were lost. The two boats left reached the coast of Siberia. Two men were sent out to reach help. They staggered into a native camp. Search parties set out, but they were too late. After many months the bodies of De Long and his men were discovered.

Another expedition set sail for the North Pole in 1881. This, too, ended in *disaster,* with only seven survivors. In 1893 a Norwegian party got closer to the Pole than any earlier group, but the Pole itself remained unexplored. This group determined that there was no land at the North Pole.

The year 1900 saw a race for the Pole. Explorers of several nations hoped to plant their country's flag there. The best hope of the United States was Robert E. Peary. Peary had studied the problem for 20 years. He had made many practice trips to the Arctic to prepare himself for a race to the Pole.

On all these trips, Peary had traveled with his aide, Matthew Henson. Peary had first met Henson in a shop in Washington. This meeting was most important for both men. Peary hired Henson and took him on a survey trip in Nicaragua. They stayed together for a great many years.

David Mountfield, who writes about the Arctic, explained: "Henson was to accompany him on all his future expeditions and to prove a man of courage and physical resource matching Peary, his senior by 7 years. The Eskimos considered him their equal as hunter and dog-driver." Mountfield added that Peary and Henson "were close comrades, entirely dependent on each other in numerous situations of extreme danger."

Henson also worked well with the Eskimos and understood their language.

In a 1906 expedition, Peary got to within 170 miles of the Pole, but he had to turn back in his ship, the *Roosevelt.* On this trip Matthew Henson showed his great strength and skill. As Russell Owen, another writer, said, "Henson was selected to make the trail because of his skill as a dog driver. His sledges were light and he could travel fast. Then came the others. . . . At the end of each march, Henson made an igloo of snow, which was used by the others who followed him."

Henson's strength and skill helped Peary on the greatest adventure of all: the successful journey to the North Pole.

The 1908 expedition had seven Americans: Peary, Henson, and five others. The party also included 17 Eskimos and 133 dogs. Peary's ship, the *Roosevelt,* also took part in this famous voyage. The party adopted the plan used by mountain climbers. A large group would act as a support group for a small team. The smaller team would be used for the final push to the Pole.

The complete party traveled across snow and ice to a point within 133 miles of the Pole. On April 1, 1909, it was time to split the party. The last of the support groups turned back. In the final assault team were Peary, Matthew Henson, and four Eskimos. They set out with high spirits for the final sprint.

Many of the early expeditions had had bad luck. "In many ways," wrote Russell Owen, "Peary's last trip, the journey to the Pole, was the easiest he had ever made, for this time luck was with him."

The final party left soon after midnight on April 2. The sun was up for 24 hours, and the weather was clear. The group hoped to average at least 25 miles a day. They did even better.

As Owen explained, "Peary's feet had been frostbitten many years before, and walking was difficult. He always tried to walk some distance alone before the sledge caught up with him. He thus hoped to keep his legs and feet in good condition. He often rode on the sledge, but near the end of a day's march, he'd get off and walk."

Because the party was so far north, the ice was in good condition. It was mostly unbroken. At times, though, the party came to a break in the ice. The members would have to pick their way across moving ice cakes. They would have to find a way for dogs and sledges to follow. There were some rough places in the ice, but these could be crossed.

The feeling of excitement grew as the party came closer to the Pole. But there was a last challenge. As Russell Owen wrote, "The day before they reached the Pole, the sky became overcast, and everything around them was bathed in a gray light that cast no shadows. It was like traveling in a bowl of milk. And it was depressing. But Peary pushed on so rapidly that in twelve hours he made thirty miles."

On April 6, Peary knew he had reached the area of the Pole.

There is no natural marker at the North Pole! Its position must be determined by measurement. Peary made the necessary observations with his sextant, a navigator's instrument. He determined that the party had reached 90 degrees latitude—the North Pole. Peary wanted to be sure he had reached the exact spot. He walked back and forth across the area for several miles. At the point he thought to be the Pole, the party built an igloo. The happy group planted an American flag on top of it. There is a picture, taken by Peary, of Matthew Henson holding a flag at the North Pole. He was one of the first six men to reach the Pole, and the first black man.

Though this was the last trip for Peary, Henson and Peary remained good friends. They had been together on each of Peary's eight Arctic trips. They had faced danger together for 23 years. Peary was recognized as the discoverer of the North Pole, but Henson helped make the discovery possible. Peary said of Henson, "I can't get along without him."

Henson won many honors in later life. He became a member of the Explorers Club and received a silver medal from the U.S. Navy. He received honorary degrees from Howard University and Morgan College. When he died at the age of 89, the press recalled his all-important role in exploring the North Pole.

UNDERSTANDING WHAT YOU HAVE READ

Finding Another Title

1. Another good title for this selection might be (a) The North Pole (b) The Story of Exploration (c) Franklin and De Long: Two Polar Heroes (d) Matthew Henson's Role in Polar History.

Getting the Main Idea

2. Which of the following best states the main idea of the selection?
   (a) Getting to the North Pole required strength, courage, and good fortune.
   (b) The 1906 expedition was the most important trip in the history of polar exploration.
   (c) Matthew Henson lived to a ripe old age.
   (d) Robert E. Peary didn't fully know the value of Matthew Henson.

Finding Details

3. Without question, the first person to sail in true polar waters was **(a)** Ottar **(b)** Pytheas **(c)** St. Brendan **(d)** Eric the Red.
4. The Franklin expedition set out in **(a)** 1844 **(b)** 1879 **(c)** 1881 **(d)** 1893.
5. The ship the *Jeannette* took part in **(a)** the Franklin expedition **(b)** the search for Sir John Franklin **(c)** the De Long expedition **(d)** Peary's 1906 expedition.
6. The leader who thought he would get close to the Pole by drifting with pack ice was **(a)** Robert E. Peary **(b)** Sir John Franklin **(c)** Ottar **(d)** Lieutenant De Long.
7. Peary first met Henson **(a)** in Nicaragua **(b)** in Washington **(c)** in Greenland **(d)** at the North Cape.
8. The person who worked well with Eskimos and interpreted their language was **(a)** De Long **(b)** Henson **(c)** Peary **(d)** Mountfield.
9. Peary first got within 170 miles of the Pole **(a)** before he met Henson **(b)** by 1900 **(c)** in 1906 **(d)** in 1908.
10. Russell Owen **(a)** is a member of the Explorers Club **(b)** was a member of the 1908 expedition **(c)** suggested a plan **(d)** is a writer.

Making Inferences

11. We may assume that the North Cape is **(a)** not as far north as Iceland **(b)** within the Arctic Circle **(c)** ice-free all year long **(d)** thickly populated.

12. The Norse were most likely **(a)** very good sailors **(b)** the first to set foot at the North Pole **(c)** interested in reaching the North Pole **(d)** very frightened.

13. The reason so many nineteenth-century trips to the Arctic failed is that **(a)** the leaders didn't fully understand the dangers **(b)** the members of the parties failed to work well together **(c)** the ships were not sound **(d)** the crews wanted more money.

14. Some explorers hoped to reach the North Pole first because of their **(a)** plans to write a book **(b)** patriotism **(c)** need for money **(d)** friends in the Explorers Club.

15. Matthew Henson has been called *resourceful*. Most likely this means he **(a)** had great wealth **(b)** had a hot temper but controlled it well **(c)** was interesting as a person **(d)** knew what to do in many different kinds of situations.

Predicting What Happens Next

16. After the 1908 expedition, **(a)** Peary tried to climb Mount Everest **(b)** other parties tried to reach the South Pole **(c)** nations lost all interest in the polar areas **(d)** the ice around the pole melted to allow a ship to reach the area.

Deciding on the Order of Events

17. The following events are scrambled. Arrange them in proper order, as they happened. Use letters only.
    (a) Sir John Franklin sets out for the north.
    (b) Matthew Henson reaches the North Pole.
    (c) Eric the Red sets up colonies on Greenland.
    (d) Lieutenant De Long begins his trip.

Inferring Attitude

18. The attitude of David Mountfield (page 139) toward Matthew Henson is one of **(a)** uncertainty **(b)** admiration **(c)** curiosity **(d)** fear.

Separating Facts from Opinions

For each of the following, tell whether the statement is a fact (*F*) or an opinion (*O*).
19. Matthew Henson was the first black person to reach the North Pole.
20. The Greek mariner Pytheas was as skillful a sailor as Ottar.

Understanding Words from Context

21. Pictures from these space flights stir the imagination and *entice* us to further exploration.
    Entice (137) means **(a)** lead on **(b)** scold **(c)** discourage **(d)** condemn.
22. Yet as long as a challenge *persists*, men and women will keep trying.
    Persists (137) means **(a)** resists **(b)** continues **(c)** disappears **(d)** happens.
23. The *quest* for a direct route from Europe to China increased interest in the Arctic.
    Quest (137) means **(a)** conquest **(b)** success **(c)** failure **(d)** search.

24. No one survived: first Franklin died; then his crew *perished* on a trip across the ice.
   Perished (138) means **(a)** became ill **(b)** survived **(c)** were lost **(d)** died.
25. One boat *capsized*, overturned by the sea.
   Capsized (138) means **(a)** crashed **(b)** was crushed **(c)** turned over **(d)** floated without power.

THINKING IT OVER

1. Some people still want to climb Mount Everest, even though it has been climbed many times. Success will not make the climbers rich or famous. Why would they risk their lives?
2. How did Matthew Henson prove to be a most important assistant to Peary?.
3. Water holds heat much better than land. The North Pole is in the frozen Arctic Ocean. The South Pole is in a land mass, frozen Antarctica. The South Pole is colder and more dangerous. Why?
4. Why are so many countries interested in Antarctica? What do you know about the various bases there?
5. Why do some airplanes fly over the North Pole in traveling from one continent to another? (Think of what a globe looks like.)

ANOTHER LOOK AT THE QUOTATION

What is it that pulls me away from what others call happiness, home and loved ones; why does my love for them not hold me down, root me? Games. Adventures. The unknown.

ANAÏS NIN

1. Explain the quotation in your own words.
2. Do you consider Anaïs Nin's answers good ones? Are games, adventures, and the unknown enough to keep people from their loved ones? Why or why not?
3. Would Matthew Henson have agreed with Anaïs Nin? Why or why not?
4. Do you ever daydream about a great adventure? Tell about it.

WORDS AT YOUR SERVICE—STORIES IN WORDS

This, too, ended in *disaster*, with only seven survivors. (139)

Scientists can pick up a piece of pottery in an ancient ruin and read its history. Words are like pieces of pottery. They can reveal a great deal of history, for there are fascinating stories in words.

The word *disaster* tells us about our history, our superstitions, our beliefs, and ourselves. You may recognize *aster*. The word meant *star* in the original Greek. You see *aster* in *astronomy, astrology, astronaut,* and *asteroid.* All these have something to do with *star.*

If we separate the parts, *dis* and *aster,* and check the dictionary, we learn that *disaster* means *evil star*. What does *disaster* have to do with an evil star?

People long believed that the stars influence our lives. Astrology, the study of these influences, is still popular today. If something worked out badly, people thought that the stars were to blame. Thus a disaster, an unhappy event, could be blamed on the stars. The expression *ill-starred* suggests the same idea. For instance, we could

say, "The Franklin expedition was an ill-starred venture."
The words in column A are taken from the selection.
The expressions in column B give brief histories of the
words in column A. Match the selections. You may use
your dictionary to help you.

A	B
1. mariner (137)	a. person who lives
2. survivor (139)	b. leaping against
3. courage (139)	c. person of the sea
4. assault (140)	d. pushed down
5. depressing (141)	e. having a heart

SACAJAWEA:

Guide to the West

*Before I judge my neighbor, let me walk
a mile in his moccasins.*

SIOUX PROVERB

April 11 is not a national holiday. But it does mark an important date. On that date in 1803, the French foreign minister approached Robert R. Livingston, the American minister to France.

"What will America give for all of the Louisiana Territory?" Livingston was surprised, but he did not let the opportunity slide. The Louisiana Territory was a land as large as all of the United States at that time. It extended from what is now Louisiana in the south to parts of what is now Montana. It included a vast area between the Mississippi River and the Rockies.

Why were the French willing to give up this land? There were difficulties between the French and the Spanish and the French and the English. The French felt that they might not be able to defend this region. Napoleon, the French leader, decided to get out at a good time.

The United States paid $15 million to France, and the new territory was joined to the land east of the Mississippi. This purchase opened up the land to the west to new settlers. Pioneers began to cross the Mississippi River. The Louisiana Purchase made a *significant* contribution to the growth of the new nation.

The new land was not well explored, however. President Thomas Jefferson wanted a land route to the Pacific Ocean. He also hoped to lay claim to the Oregon territory in the far northwest. He decided to send an expedition on a journey of exploration. For that purpose he called on his private secretary, Captain Meriwether Lewis.

Lewis selected William Clark as his partner in command and began the preparations. They chose and trained men during the winter of 1803–1804. In May 1804 they started their journey at a point just across the Mississippi from St. Louis. St. Louis is important because the Missouri River runs into the Mississippi River at that point. The men set out up the Missouri just a year after Louisiana was purchased.

That fall the Lewis and Clark Expedition decided to spend the winter among the Mandan Indians. Their winter quarters were near present-day Bismarck, North Dakota.

It was here that Lewis and Clark made a lucky decision. They hired a French Canadian trapper and his Indian wife to act as guides. In addition, the Indian wife, named Sacajawea*, could help in contacting other Indians and speaking to them. The name *Sacajawea* may mean *Bird Woman*.

On February 11, 1805, Sacajawea gave birth to a baby boy. He was named Jean Baptiste. Little Jean went along with the expedition. His presence was a help. It showed other Indians that the expedition was not a war party.

Sacajawea was a Shoshone Indian. She had been captured by other Indians many years earlier and brought to their camp. There she was sold to the trapper and became his wife. Since she was a Shoshone, she was especially valuable to Lewis and Clark. The expedition was heading into Shoshone country.

The expedition set out on April 7, 1805. More than two years passed before it returned successfully to St. Louis. These two years were important in the growth of the United States.

The story of Sacajawea is filled with praise for her efforts. She not only helped contact other Indians. She helped the men survive. She found herbs and roots for medicines and food. She used her knowledge of the land to guide the expedition through strange and unfamiliar regions. She was an important member of the party and often proved her worth.

Once, for example, she helped save many supplies. Her husband was not a good sailor, but he took his turn piloting one of the boats. A sudden wind struck the boat and

---

*sak-uh-juh-WEE-uh

turned it partially around. The sail went out of control, and the boat turned over on its side. Water began pouring in. Sacajawea's husband was of little use, and the other men finally saved the boat. During all these troubles, Sacajawea sat waist-deep in water. She kept calm, quietly recovering most of the supplies that floated past her. Lewis praised her highly for her help.

The explorers spent the next two days drying out. They had lost some items like medicine, gunpowder, and garden seeds. But Sacajawea had saved some of the most important books, paper, and trade goods.

The party had many adventures and faced many dangers. Once a grizzly bear started to attack Lewis but turned away at the last moment. Rattlesnakes were an ever-present danger. The land itself presented problems.

In June the expedition reached the Great Falls of the Missouri. The explorers could hear the roar of the water from seven miles away. When they arrived at the falls, they were stunned. How could they pass this obstacle? They decided to carry all their supplies and boats overland, but the job was staggering.

Meanwhile Sacajawea had been seriously ill for a week. She was feverish and near death. Then, fortunately, someone brought water from a sulphur spring nearby. This proved to be the right medicine, and Sacajawea recovered enough to help with the *portage,* as the overland hike was called.

The party had usually made 18 miles a day on the river. The portage would take two weeks for the same distance. The largest boat could not be carried and was left behind. The smaller boat could not hold all the supplies. Therefore some supplies had to be left behind also. These supplies would help on the way back.

The weather did not always cooperate. On June 29 a violent storm struck. Rain and hailstones battered the party. One man was knocked to the ground. Some others had bloodied heads. Clark and Sacajawea, among others, were at the river when the storm broke. They thought they would be safe in a gully, but the water rose quickly. The suddenly rising water nearly drowned the party. Clark helped Sacajawea and her baby to higher ground, barely ahead of the rising water. Clark lost his knapsack, gun, tomahawk, umbrella, powderhorn, and compass. Fortunately, he recovered one item the next day—the compass.

On July 22, 1805, Sacajawea thought the countryside began to look familiar. She said that her tribe lived in this vast area. She wasn't sure exactly where. Since leaving Fort Mandan in April, the party had not seen an Indian. They had seen abandoned campsites and smoke signals—but no Indians.

On August 8, Sacajawea raised the spirits of everyone. She spotted a familiar landmark. A week later, a party with Clark in charge set out ahead of the others. Sacajawea was in the lead. Within a mile, Sacajawea stopped and danced with happiness. Some mounted Indians were approaching. They were Shoshone, her own people.

A meeting was called with the Indians. Since Sacajawea knew the language, she was brought in to help *interpret*. A peace pipe was smoked. Then Sacajawea gave a cry of joy. She recognized the chief as her brother. She kept to her task of interpreting, but she had to stop several times. Tears of joy were streaming down her cheeks.

The meeting was a success. The expedition members and the Indians agreed to help each other. The Indians supplied the party with needed horses. Though she rejoiced in the reunion, Sacajawea decided to continue with the expedition. She had a duty to the party. It was still a long way to the Pacific Ocean.

On the next leg of the journey, the party met many other Indian tribes. The names are particularly colorful:

the Flathead, the Nez Percé ("pierced nose"), the Chinook, the Walla Walla. With help from Sacajawea and good common sense, Lewis and Clark got along well with the Indian tribes they met. They found them friendly, interested in trade, and helpful in giving directions.

The expedition reached the area of the Pacific Ocean in November. Lewis and Clark realized that they couldn't return over the mountains till spring, and so they built a fort. They had a merry Christmas celebration, but their joy didn't last long. The winter was *wretched*—bitterly cold and damp.

The book *Lewis and Clark,* edited by Robert G. Ferris, reports, "From November 4, 1805, to March 25, 1806, rain fell every day except 12 and only half of those were clear. The dampness damaged the gunpowder, and *mildewed* and rotted clothing, bedding, and trade goods, which had to be dried by the fire. Many of the men suffered from rheumatism, colds, and influenza. Fleas pestered everyone."

The party couldn't wait for the spring.

In January, Indians reported that the body of a whale had been washed ashore. Sacajawea again showed her interest in nature. She requested that she and her son be taken to see the whale. She also wanted to see the "great waters" she had traveled so far to reach. By the time the party arrived at the site, the Indians had stripped the meat and blubber. But the 105-foot skeleton was an impressive sight.

The party set April 1 as the date for returning to the East. The rains were so disheartening that the date was moved to March 20. Heavy rains caused a few days' delay, but on March 22 an advance hunting party finally left camp.

The trip east was even more difficult in some ways than the trip west. The boat had to fight against the current on the Columbia River. High water elsewhere forced a change of plans. Several times Sacajawea proved her value as a member of the expedition. Her knowledge of herbs, for example, helped fight illness on the trip. Her knowledge of trailblazing helped guide the party.

In the Nez Percé village, Lewis and Clark met some old and new friends: Twisted Hair, Cutnose, and Broken Arm. Then, because the purpose of the journey was exploration, Lewis and Clark took separate routes back to St. Louis. Sacajawea and her husband stayed on in what is now North Dakota.

For Sacajawea the journey had been a wonderful experience. She had seen many strange new lands. She had met people of different races and tribes. She had come to understand how much alike all people are, in spite of obvious differences. She had given much and received much.

What happened to Sacajawea afterward? There is evidence that she brought her son to St. Louis in 1809. She may have left her son with Clark to be educated. Some sources say she died on December 20, 1812, at Fort Lisa. This is near present-day Omaha, Nebraska.

There is another story, though, that is more to our liking. There was an old Indian woman living among the Shoshone of Wyoming in 1875. She claimed to be Sacajawea. She died in 1884, which would have made Sacajawea nearly 100 years old.

No one knows the true story, but there is a bronze statue on the Capitol grounds in Bismarck, North Dakota. It shows a lovely Indian woman with a small child on her back. She looks toward the land she loved. This is truly Sacajawea.

UNDERSTANDING WHAT YOU HAVE READ

Finding Another Title

1. Another good title for this selection might be (a) Conquering the West (b) The Louisiana Purchase (c) The Role of Sacajawea in the Lewis and Clark Expedition (d) Lewis and Clark and the Indians of the American Northwest.

Getting the Main Idea

2. The Lewis and Clark Expedition (a) overcame dangers and hardships, often with the help of an Indian guide (b) had as its purpose the removal of foreign powers from the Louisiana Territory (c) failed in its major purpose (d) had an easy journey to the Pacific.

Finding Details

3. The United States purchased the Louisiana Territory from the (a) Indians (b) English (c) French (d) Spanish.

4. By the Louisiana Purchase, the United States (a) won California (b) surprised the French (c) set back settlements by years (d) doubled its size.

5. After the Louisiana Purchase, the Lewis and Clark Expedition set out (a) the following year (b) three years later (c) from Omaha (d) in spite of President Jefferson's opposition.

6. The tribe that Sacajawea belonged to was the (a) Flathead (b) Chinook (c) Nez Percé (d) Shoshone.

7. The Lewis and Clark Expedition had to carry boats and supplies across land because of (a) the Great Falls (b) a sudden storm (c) the drying up of a river (d) an attack by the French.
8. A severe storm struck the party on (a) April 7 (b) June 29 (c) July 22 (d) March 25.
9. The party left their fort on the West Coast more than a week early because of (a) Lewis's dream (b) a message from President Jefferson (c) the birth of Sacajawea's son (d) the weather.
10. All the following Indians are mentioned EXCEPT (a) Broken Arm (b) Sitting Bull (c) Cutnose (d) Twisted Hair.

Making Inferences

11. Napoleon probably decided to sell the Louisiana Territory because he was afraid he (a) was getting ill (b) would make enemies in the United States (c) would lose the territory anyway (d) didn't know the boundaries of the territory.
12. Thomas Jefferson chose Meriwether Lewis because (a) the two were related (b) Jefferson knew Lewis and had faith in him (c) Lewis had arranged for the Louisiana Purchase (d) Robert R. Livingston was not available.
13. Lewis and Clark (a) chose Sacajawea because no one else was available (b) did not expect to reach the Pacific Ocean (c) counted on the help of the Shoshone Indians (d) disagreed with each other nearly every day.
14. The "great waters" referred to on page 154 are the (a) Great Salt Lake (b) Missouri River (c) Pacific Ocean (d) Great Falls.

15. Good words to describe Sacajawea in difficult circumstances are **(a)** *calm* and *courageous* **(b)** *nervous* and *cautious* **(c)** *cruel* and *clever* **(d)** *sweet* and *easily led.*

Predicting What Happens Next

16. At the conclusion of the expedition, Lewis and Clark probably **(a)** set out at once to retrace their steps **(b)** made a fortune on trade goods from the Indians **(c)** set up shop in St. Louis **(d)** reported to President Jefferson.

Deciding on the Order of Events

17. The following events are scrambled. Arrange them in proper order, as they happened. Use letters only.
(a) Sacajawea sees the skeleton of a whale.
(b) Sacajawea sees her brother, a Shoshone chief.
(c) Lewis and Clark set out on their expedition.
(d) Sacajawea brings her son to St. Louis.

Inferring Tone

18. The description of the winter of 1805–1806 (154) gives the impression of **(a)** a happy challenge **(b)** an interesting change **(c)** complete misery **(d)** mild discomfort.

Separating Facts from Opinions

For each of the following, tell whether the statement is a fact (*F*) or an opinion (*O*).
19. Sacajawea was the most important member of the Lewis and Clark Expedition.

20. Sacajawea and her husband left the expedition in what is now North Dakota.

Understanding Words from Context

21. The Louisiana Purchase made a *significant* contribution to the growth of the new nation.
    Significant (150) means   **(a)** temporary   **(b)** slim   **(c)** well advertised   **(d)** important.
22. They could no longer travel by water. Sacajawea recovered enough to help with the *portage*.
    Portage   (152)   means   **(a)** mining   operation   **(b)** fishing with a net   **(c)** overland carry   **(d)** map reading.
23. Since Sacajawea knew the language, she was brought in to help *interpret*.
    Interpret (153) means   **(a)** explain in another language   **(b)** plan for the next operation   **(c)** exchange goods with the Indians   **(d)** find a solution to problems.
24. The winter was *wretched*—bitterly cold and damp.
    Wretched (154) means   **(a)** exciting   **(b)** miserable   **(c)** chilly   **(d)** too humid.
25. Ferris reports, "The dampness damaged the gunpowder, and *mildewed* and rotted clothing."
    Mildewed (154) means   **(a)** cleaned   **(b)** made more powerful   **(c)** covered with a fungus   **(d)** dried.

THINKING IT OVER

1. Was the Louisiana Purchase a good bargain for the United States? Explain.
2. In what ways did Sacajawea help the Lewis and Clark Expedition?

3. What was the attitude of the Shoshone Indians toward the expedition?
4. On what occasions did Sacajawea show her courage? Tell about them.
5. Would you have enjoyed being a member of the Lewis and Clark Expedition? Why or why not?
6. Are small discomforts sometimes as damaging as serious problems? Explain. Give examples from your own experiences.

ANOTHER LOOK AT THE QUOTATION

*Before I judge my neighbor, let me walk
a mile in his moccasins.*

SIOUX PROVERB

1. Explain the quotation in your own words.
2. Do you think the advice sound? Explain.
3. The members of the Lewis and Clark Expedition got along with the Indians whom they met. Did they follow the advice of the proverb? Explain.
4. Would some world problems be solved if all nations tried to see the other nations' point of view? Explain.

WORDS AT YOUR SERVICE—WORD ELEMENTS

The weather did not always *cooperate*.

If you remember the word *disaster* (page 139), you recall it consisted of two parts, *dis* and *aster*. Many words contain more than one element.

Notice that the word *cooperate* (152) is made up of three parts: *co, oper,* and *ate.* These parts have names. *Co* is a prefix, a letter or group of letters added to the beginning of a word or word root. *Oper* is a root, the base of the word. *Ate* is a suffix, a letter or group of letters added to the end of a word or word root.

The root usually carries the central meaning. Here, *oper* comes from a Latin word meaning *work.* The prefix, *co,* comes from a Latin word meaning *together.* The suffix, *ate,* comes from a Latin word meaning *make* or *act.* If you put the parts together, you can see that *cooperate* means *act to work together.*

Not all words have all three parts. *Command* (150) has a prefix, *com,* and a root, *mand,* but no suffix. *Dampness* (154) has a root, *damp,* and a suffix, *ness,* but no prefix. A great many words have neither prefix nor suffix: *book, fall, right, spend, use,* and *west.*

1. Point out the prefix and the root in each of the following words. Use your dictionary to help you.

    compass, contact, control, interpret, overland

2. Point out the suffix and the root in each of the following words. Use your dictionary to help you.

    claimed, friendly, helped, helpful, lovely

3. Point out the prefix, the root, and the suffix in each of the following words. Use your dictionary to help you.

    addition, important, impressive, included, reported

SALLY RIDE:

First American Woman in Space

*Space is a new ocean, and I believe the
United States must sail upon it.*
                    JOHN F. KENNEDY

The space shuttle rests on the launching pad. The countdown to blast-off continues: 30 seconds, 29 . . . 3, 2, 1. All the spectators are hushed. There is a mighty roar and a brilliant blast of flame as the shuttle slowly rises from the pad. The spectators are excited and relieved. The launch is a success. What is the blast-off like inside the shuttle? "The engines light, the solids light, and all of a sudden you know you're *going*. It's overwhelming. There is nothing like it. The simulators give you the noise and the vibration, but the sensation is not the thrust. It's psychological. It *literally* overwhelms you."

This is Sally Ride, first American woman astronaut, describing the moment of blast-off in the space shuttle *Challenger* in June 1983. Simulators are training devices to prepare astronauts for experiences in the space shuttle. But as Sally says, not even simulators can prepare an astronaut for that first lift-off into space.

Preparing for this moment takes a long time. Sally was accepted into the space program in 1978, along with five other women. For five years she went through the difficult training course preparing her for the shuttle's leaving its home on Earth and soaring into space. But all the work was worthwhile.

The flight with Sally Ride was the seventh shuttle mission. It was the second for the *Challenger*. The *Columbia* had completed five earlier missions. *Challenger 2* was one of the program's most successful missions.

After the excitement of blast-off, the shuttle crew settled down to work. There were four other astronauts in addition to Sally. The commander of the mission was Robert Crippen, the pilot of the first shuttle in 1981. The pilot of this seventh mission was Frederick Hauck. John Fabian, like Sally, was a mission specialist. Norman Thagard was the spacecraft's doctor. Since no one showed signs of illness, Thagard could do other tasks.

This space mission lasted 146 hours. It did more than any earlier shuttle mission. It put two satellites into space. It ran several experiments. It *operated* the robot arm to put a satellite into space and then get it back.

That experience was helpful later. In April 1984, members of the *Challenger* captured, repaired, and returned a *disabled* satellite to orbit. This was the first time a disabled satellite had been repaired in space.

Sally Ride played an important role. She helped release the two communications satellites. She ran several experiments on board. She added a great deal of humor. Once when working out on the treadmill in space, she said that she was "probably one of the few people to run across the Indian Ocean."

It was not all work in space. There was time for fun, too. President Ronald Reagan had sent the astronauts some jelly beans as a fun gift. While they were in space, Sally and her fellow astronauts let the jelly beans loose. They floated in air, in zero gravity. The astronauts tried to catch them with open mouths. This trick is a lot harder than catching a peanut thrown into the air!

Only one thing went wrong on this highly successful flight. The *Challenger* was supposed to land at Florida's Kennedy Space Center. It had taken off from that base six days earlier. If the shuttle could land at Kennedy, it would be the first to complete a truly round trip. All other missions had begun in Florida and ended in California.

As the time for the landing arrived, the news from Florida was bad. Fog and moisture presented some dangers to the *Challenger*'s insulating tiles. Therefore, the *Challenger* was directed to Edwards Air Force Base in the Mojave Desert. The dry air of the desert would present no problems.

If you have seen a shuttle landing on television, you may think landing it is easy. It's not.

On the ninety-seventh orbit, Commander Crippen fired twin braking rockets high above the Indian Ocean. He turned off the automatic pilot at 78,000 feet. From there on down, the lives of the astronauts depended on his skill. Crippen took *manual* control and made a wide sweeping turn. This would bring the shuttle in line with the runway. As *Newsweek* magazine wrote, "He had just one chance to get it right: the shuttle operates like a glider during its descent, with no engines to power up for a second try."

The *Challenger* glided to a perfect landing. The mission was completed.

There was a party to welcome the astronauts, but unfortunately it was somewhere else. Back at Kennedy Space Center, the crowds had gathered for the landing. Thousands rose before dawn to watch the *Challenger* come to rest. Space fans wore T-shirts saying, "Ride, Sally Ride." Sally Ride's father and mother had flown all the way from California to watch the historic event. Her father said, "We live only a hundred miles from the California runway. We could have stayed home."

Some were disappointed, but the general mood was one of *jubilation*. Another shuttle mission had succeeded.

The seventh mission was historic for many reasons. It had performed many space experiments without a problem. The crew had stayed healthy, avoiding the space sickness that bothers some astronauts. Perhaps, most important of all, a woman had proved herself able to perform the tasks in space.

The astronaut-training program had no doubts about the ability of women. As Sally said, "The attitude of both men and women in the astronaut program was not, were you a man or woman, but could you do the job?" Yet many people wondered whether the experiment would turn out well. Many old false views and superstitions rose to the surface.

In an interview Sally was asked, "Why do you think you were chosen for the flight?" She replied simply, "Because I knew what I was doing. I was trained as an expert in using the shuttle arm to *deploy* satellites—and I still am." But the astronaut cannot be too limited a specialist. Sally is not. She added, "You have to be able to meet the demands of any flight."

Sally is usually quite calm. When she talks about the space flight, however, she reveals her feelings. She was asked, "What was the high point of your life?"

"Oh, the shuttle flight. Absolutely."

The interviewer asked, "Was it exciting, thrilling?"

Sally replied, "No. It's not that it's exciting. It's not thrilling. It's, it's . . . unique. An experience that no one can have on the ground. Absolutely fantastic."

Sally is popular with all the people she works with. Jim McNearny is a veteran photographer at the Kennedy Space Center. Through the years he has met and worked with most of the astronauts. He recalls Sally Ride as warm, friendly, bright, modest, and outgoing. She was a good choice for her important role.

Sally is an extraordinary person in other ways. She has a sound educational background. She started out as a major in English literature, and earned a bachelor's degree. Then her interests changed. She earned a bachelor's degree in physics as well. Then she went on to earn a doctor's degree in physics, a most difficult achievement.

Her life was changed by an ad in the school newspaper. The ad asked for astronaut candidates. She sent in a postcard . . . and her world was changed forever. There were 8,300 applicants, both men and women. Sally was chosen.

Sally's personal life is not run-of-the-mill. When she married fellow astronaut Steve Hawley, she flew her plane to the wedding. They were married in the backyard of

Steve's parents' house in Kansas. When she went into space, she took her wedding ring with her.

Steve had his turn in space later. On August 30, 1984, the *Discovery*, the third of the nation's shuttle craft, had its first flight. Steve was aboard.

Sally was more than just another astronaut. She says, "We all knew, both the men and women astronauts, that it was extremely important that a woman go up in the shuttle. She should be a role model, and that would be important. I didn't particularly care that I was the role model, but I thought it was important that somebody be."

Sally handled herself well after the first flight. She remained modest, although she became an instant celebrity. A school in Texas was named after her. She looked forward, however, to being "just another astronaut."

Sally was a pioneer in space. Others were to follow. On August 30, 1983, the *Challenger* began its third mission. On this historic journey, Air Force Lieutenant Colonel Guion Bluford became the first black American astronaut to be carried into space.

Like Sally Ride, Colonel Bluford joined the astronaut program in 1978. Also like Sally, he had a sound educational background for his role in space. He had always been fascinated by airplanes. Even in high school he decided on a career in aerospace engineering. He received a degree from Penn State University and completed the Air Force ROTC program. This program, which he took while he was in college, prepared him for his career in the Air Force. In 1966–1977 he flew 144 missions in Vietnam.

This record wasn't enough. He logged more than 3,000 hours as a jet pilot. He completed his training by earning a doctor's degree in aerospace engineering. With this education, Colonel Bluford could have made more money in private industry. But he chose to stay on as an astronaut. He was ready. As he said, "The space program was an expansion of what I was already doing."

As time goes by, more and more barriers fall. After Sally came Judith A. Resnick, the second American woman in space. She took part in the first flight of the *Discovery* from August 30 to September 5, 1984. And after Guion Bluford came mission specialist Ronald McNair. He flew on the fourth *Challenger* mission, which took off February 3, 1984.

Shuttle crews included more and more men and women of different backgrounds. On the October 6–13, 1984, mission, Kathryn D. Sullivan became the first American woman to walk in space. Her training had been as a geologist and oceanographer. A month later Dr. Anna Fisher, a physician, joined the shuttle crew. Major Ellison S. Onizuka flew on the *Discovery* mission that blasted off on January 4, 1985.

Twenty-four shuttle missions had been successful, but tragedy struck suddenly. On January 28, 1986, the shuttle *Challenger* was again on the launch pad. The astronauts included three already mentioned: Judith Resnick, Ronald McNair, and Ellison Onizuka. Dick Scobee, Michael Smith, and Gregory Jarvis made up the rest of the crew, along with Christa McAuliffe, the first teacher on a shuttle mission.

Shortly after liftoff, the *Challenger* exploded, killing all crew members. The tragedy shocked the nation and temporarily halted the space program. But the families of the lost astronauts urged the nation to proceed with the space program. Otherwise the seven might have died in vain.

Heroism has always risen above danger.

UNDERSTANDING WHAT YOU HAVE READ

Finding Another Title

1. Another good title for this selection might be **(a)** How the Shuttle Operates **(b)** The U.S. Space Program **(c)** A Successful Mission **(d)** Pioneer American Woman Astronaut.

Getting the Main Idea

2. Sally Ride was **(a)** a good choice for her important role **(b)** an outstanding scientist **(c)** disappointed in the role she played **(d)** a flier as well as an astronaut.

Finding Details

3. The second *Challenger* mission took off in **(a)** 1981 **(b)** 1982 **(c)** 1983 **(d)** 1984.
4. The commander of Sally's shuttle mission was **(a)** Norman   Thagard **(b)** Robert   Crippen **(c)** Frederick Hauck **(d)** Sally herself.
5. The jelly beans on the shuttle mission were the gift of **(a)** Sally's mother **(b)** John Fabian **(c)** Anna Fisher **(d)** Ronald Reagan.
6. Jim McNearny is **(a)** an astronaut **(b)** a photographer **(c)** a news reporter **(d)** a mechanic.
7. Sally Ride's space training began **(a)** in the same year as Guion Bluford's **(b)** while she was still in high school **(c)** in the Mojave Desert **(d)** in 1980.

8. Steve Hawley is (a) a television announcer (b) a ground-control engineer (c) Sally's husband (d) a writer about the space program.
9. Guion Bluford was an officer in the (a) Army (b) Navy (c) Air Force (d) Marines.
10. Anna Fisher is (a) a writer (b) an engineer (c) an army officier (d) a physician.

Making Inferences

11. The preparation of astronauts may be described as (a) brief but thorough (b) long and demanding (c) boring and dull (d) wasteful.
12. Sally Ride's *Challenger* flight may best be described as (a) bothered by space sickness (b) unusually successful (c) less successful than the previous flights (d) partly spoiled by disagreements among the crew.
13. The *Challenger 2* mission (a) went along on schedule without any changes (b) disappointed everyone (c) supported the place of women in the space program (d) returned a disabled satellite to orbit.
14. On shuttle flights a mission specialist (a) is usually made the commander (b) has a particular kind of job to do (c) acts as the craft's doctor (d) is also a trained pilot.
15. Astronauts who have flown shuttle missions probably (a) believe in the importance of space exploration (b) want to train others to fly (c) are content to stay on the ground in future flights (d) would like to become movie stars.

Predicting What Happens Next

16. After the successful 1984 flights, **(a)** a woman was made head of a 1985 mission **(b)** Kathryn D. Sullivan went into private industry **(c)** the space agency stopped taking applications from women **(d)** other women were chosen for shuttle flights.

Deciding on the Order of Events

17. The following events are scrambled. Arrange them in proper order, as they happened. Use letters only.
(a) Colonel Bluford flies into space.
(b) Sally applies for a job as astronaut.
(c) Steve Hawley flies on a shuttle mission.
(d) Kathryn D. Sullivan walks in space.

Inferring Tone

18. Sally Ride's description of the blast-off (163) can best be described as **(a)** surprisingly calm **(b)** controlled but excited **(c)** bored **(d)** not happy.

Separating Facts from Opinions

For each of the following, tell whether the statement is a fact (*F*) or an opinion (*O*).
19. Each shuttle flight should have at least two women astronauts aboard.
20. Robert Crippen was a pilot on one flight, the commander of another.

Understanding Words from Context

21. Sally says that the take-off *"literally* overwhelms you." In other words, you truly know amazement. *Literally* (163) means (a) suddenly (b) surprisingly (c) really (d) unfortunately.
22. Crew members captured, repaired, and returned a *disabled* satellite to orbit. *Disabled* (164) means (a) not working (b) complicated (c) mechanical (d) unattached.
23. Crippen turned off the automatic pilot; he took *manual* control and made a wide sweeping turn. *Manual* (165) means (a) confident (b) by hand (c) automatic (d) by training.
24. Some were disappointed, but the general mood was one of *jubilation*. *Jubilation* (165) means (a) lack of control (b) sadness (c) expectation (d) joy.
25. "I was trained in using the shuttle arm to *deploy* satellites." *Deploy* (166) means (a) put into place (b) photograph on the spot (c) throw (d) look for and find.

THINKING IT OVER

1. Why was it important for a woman to be included in a shuttle mission?
2. How did Sally Ride prove she was a good choice for her pioneering role?
3. Does progress usually involve some risk? Why are people willing to accept the risk?

4. From time to time the space agency invites people to fly on a mission. If you had the chance, would you go? Tell why or why not.
5. Some people are critical of the space program. They say the money should go to solve problems on Earth. Others say that the space program does help solve Earth's problems, too. Which side of this argument are you on? Explain.
6. Goodman Ace said, "Moon rocks are OK when everyone is eating." What did he mean? On which side of the space argument would he be? Explain.
7. Explain what is meant by the quotation (165), "He had just one chance to get it right."
8. Do you support an effort to land an astronaut on the planet Mars? Explain.
9. Why is travel to even the nearest star an impossible dream at this time?
10. Lucas and Spielberg (41) deal with fantasy. The space shuttle is real. Do you prefer to read science fiction or to read about actual space achievements? Explain.

ANOTHER LOOK AT THE QUOTATION

> *Space is a new ocean, and I believe the
> United States must sail upon it.*
> JOHN F. KENNEDY

1. Explain the quotation in your own words.
2. Why did Kennedy call space an *ocean?* Was there a time when the world's oceans were as mysterious as

space? Explain. (Review pages 137–139 of the Matthew Henson chapter.)
3. Do you agree that the United States must keep trying to be strong in space? Why or why not?

WORDS AT YOUR SERVICE—COMMON LATIN ROOTS

It *operated* the robot arm to put a satellite into space and then get it back. (164)

In the last chapter (161) you met the Latin root *oper,* meaning *work.* Now the root turns up again, and here too it has the same basic meaning. *Operated* means *worked.* Knowing some Latin roots can help you figure out the meaning of new words.

You can get a feeling for some roots by seeing a lot of words with related meaning. Take the *port* words, for example. You may know *transport, import, deport,* and *porter.* In the last chapter you met *portage.* All these words have something to do with *carry.* That's the meaning of the root *port.*

Here are five additional helpful Latin roots.

Root	*Meaning*	*Example*	*Definition of the English Word*
aud	hear	*aud*ible	able to be *heard*
jac, ject	throw	pro*ject*ile	something *thrown* into the air
miss, mit	send	trans*mit*	*send* across space
mot, mov	move	de*mote*	*move* down
scrib, script	write	*scrib*ble	*write* hastily

Fill in the blank in each sentence by supplying the missing root from the list on the previous page. The number in parentheses tells you how many letters you need. Use your dictionary to help you.

EXAMPLE

Im——s are goods *carried* into a country. (4)
Insert *port*. The complete word is *imports*.

1. That piano is too heavy to *move*. It is almost im——able. (3)
2. Something that is *thrown* back is re——ed. (4)
3. Something *written* on a piece of paper is an in——ion. (6)
4. Something that is *sent* through the mails is trans——ted. (3)
5. The ——itory nerve helps us *hear*. (3)

ANOTHER LOOK

HOW MUCH DO YOU REMEMBER?

1. The two who explored lands on Earth are **(a)** Paul Newman and Sally Ride **(b)** Matthew Henson and Sacajawea **(c)** Sacajawea and Paul Newman **(d)** Sally Ride and Sacajawea.
2. The person who prepared a commercial product is **(a)** Paul Newman **(b)** Matthew Henson **(c)** Sacajawea **(d)** Sally Ride.
3. The person who traveled far overland to see the "great waters" was **(a)** Sally Ride **(b)** Paul Newman **(c)** Matthew Henson **(d)** Sacajawea.
4. Matthew Henson was a close friend of **(a)** Paul Newman **(b)** Lewis and Clark **(c)** Robert E. Peary **(d)** President McKinley.
5. The person who is interested in racing cars is **(a)** Colonel Guion Bluford **(b)** Paul Newman **(c)** Sally Ride **(d)** Robert Redford.
6. The person who said, "The engines light, the solids light, and all of a sudden you know you're *going*" was **(a)** Sir John Franklin **(b)** Matthew Henson **(c)** Paul Newman **(d)** Sally Ride.
7. All the following can be said about the movie *The Sting* EXCEPT **(a)** it has music by Scott Joplin **(b)** it stars Redford and Newman **(c)** Sally Ride

plays a very small part in it (**d**) it was a financial success.

8. In the Matthew Henson story, the journey to the North Pole was compared with (**a**) a trip to the moon (**b**) the Lewis and Clark Expedition (**c**) a trip to the Sahara Desert (**d**) the movie *Star Wars*.

9. A successful trip to the North Pole was first made by (**a**) Matthew Henson (**b**) Lieutenant George Washington De Long (**c**) William Clark (**d**) none of these.

10. Both Sally Ride and Paul Newman (**a**) are completely fearless (**b**) enjoy racing cars (**c**) seek adventure (**d**) admire Matthew Henson.

WHAT IS YOUR OPINION?

1. Which person in this unit had the most exciting adventure? Explain.

2. G. K. Chesterton once said that we can make every annoyance or inconvenience an adventure if we look at it in the right way. Suppose you can't open a stuck window. Instead of getting mad, consider the job an adventure. Try to find ways to solve the problem. Is this good advice? Explain.

3. Travel is adventure. Yet travel can be hard and even unpleasant work. Is adventure really inside our own minds?

4. Why did Matthew Henson leave the safety of his life at home to sail north? What drove him to risk his life? Would you go on an adventure if you would be risking your life? Explain.

5. Adventure movies give you experiences and don't cause you to risk your life. What adventure movies have you seen that you especially enjoy? Tell about them.

THE QUOTATION AND THE UNIT

> *My favorite thing is to go where I've never been.*
>
> DIANE ARBUS

1. Explain the quotation in your own words.
2. What are some of the places you'd like to go where you've never been?
3. Why aren't most people content to stay at home in safety? Why travel?
4. Which of our four subjects had the strangest experience? Explain.
5. Some children like to have the same story read over and over again. Some adults like to go back to the same place for a vacation, year after year. Are these people smarter than those who spend money visiting strange places? Give your point of view.

UNIT 4

CHALLENGING OLD IDEAS

Admitting error clears the score
And proves you wiser than before.
ARTHUR GUITERMAN

Old ideas die hard. Scientists had always believed that life could not exist at temperatures above 212 degrees. Then other scientists found bacteria living at over 600 degrees! The old idea had finally been proved wrong.

The subjects in this unit challenged old ideas and proved them wrong. Susan Taylor challenged the idea that black women would not support a

179

magazine devoted to their special goals and interests. She helped develop such a magazine and then challenged another idea. She proceeded to get men to read her special magazine. If they are interested, men *will* read a women's magazine.

Twyla Tharp presented many new and original ideas in modern dance. She then challenged the idea that a creator of modern dance could not succeed in classical ballet. She has done both successfully.

Lewis Thomas, in his writing, showed over and over again the error of many accepted ideas. He said, "We learn by trial and error," for that is the way of science.

Robert Goddard was a man ahead of his times. He dared to challenge the idea that rockets are merely toys. He paid the price. He was ridiculed and criticized, disregarded and insulted.

The four subjects in this unit show why it is important to test old ideas. They suggest, "Take everything with a grain of salt. Trust your own judgment and move ahead."

SUSAN L. TAYLOR:
Magazine Editor

*I would rather fail in an attempt at
something new and uncharted than
safely succeed in a repeat of something I
have done.*

A. E. HOTCHNER

Take a look at the average newsstand. What do you see? Row upon row of magazines with attractive covers and bright lettering. Each magazine is trying to get your attention. The competition is keen.

Competition has created many changes in magazines. Some of the mass-circulation magazines have lost readers. Many of the old-time giants have disappeared altogether. Others, like *Life* and the *Saturday Evening Post,* have come back in different form. Television has taken the place of some of the old general magazines.

Some critics thought that *television* would kill most magazines. The opposite is true. Magazines are doing very well. But these are not necessarily the same ones as in the past. Because people have so many interests, special magazines have become popular. These appeal to every group and every hobby.

Changes in modern living have brought about new magazines. For example, the rise of computers has brought a great many computer magazines to the stands. Each one tries to be something special, a little different from the rest. Each has its own faithful band of readers.

Then there are the special sports magazines. There are magazines devoted to football, basketball, baseball, golf, tennis, skiing, cycling, jogging, and many other popular physical activities. Magazines are devoted to health, to keeping in shape. Hunting and fishing are also covered in special sports magazines.

Are you an outdoors type? You will find camping magazines to help you set up a tent and cook a good camp meal. You will find magazines for hikers. Wildlife hobbyists have magazines for their special interests. People who like to travel have special magazines, too.

Your interests need not be active or *strenuous.* Do you have a hobby? You'll find magazines devoted to stamp collecting, chess, gardening, fashion, crafts, and cooking.

The increasing importance of science in modern life has brought about many new science magazines. Some, like *Scientific American,* are rather difficult and intended for advanced readers. Others, like *Discover,* are intended for average readers interested in science. Some magazines are devoted to science fiction.

Television and radio have brought about numerous magazines. *TV Guide,* which always battles the *Reader's Digest* for the number-one circulation spot, has special sections for each part of the country. Fans of soap operas have their own magazine.

Giant weekly news magazines still hold their readers. *Time, Newsweek,* and *U.S. News & World Report* try to explain the news and analyze events.

There are special magazines for various age groups. Children and teenagers have magazines for their interests. Other magazines, like *Field and Stream,* seem pointed toward men. Still others, like *Ms.* and *Ladies Home Journal,* are directed toward women.

The number of magazines on newsstands is staggering. Suppose you wanted to start a new magazine today? How would you begin? What special appeal would you develop? What readers would you hope to capture? What part of the market would you try to move in on? Let's follow one magazine as it began life in 1970.

The founders of *Essence* magazine decided that there was a gap on the newsstand. They thought there was no quality magazine devoted principally to the concerns of black women. An excellent magazine like *Ebony* appealed to black people in general. But there was no black women's magazine. The founders decided they'd close that gap. The first issue of *Essence* appeared in May 1970.

Fifteen years later, Ed Lewis, publisher, looked back. In the May 1985 issue of *Essence* he wrote, "We were terribly excited as we *anticipated* the birth of our first issue and had many questions." Their new magazine became a success.

That first issue of *Essence* sold 50,000 copies. In 15 years *Essence* never experienced a drop in circulation. It remained profitable. By the time of its anniversary issue in May 1985, it had developed a circulation of 800,000 and a readership of four million.

Those 15 years were not easy times, however. There were problems and disputes. In the early years some readers objected to the articles on fashion. They complained, "We need more space for the real lives of black women."

There were worries. In one year the magazine had three editors-in-chief. In 1971 Marcia Ann Gillespie took over the magazine. Under her guidance, the magazine began to find itself. In an article about the magazine, reporter Georgia Dullea wrote, "Fashion, beauty, food, health, child care, the usual women's magazine fare, was covered, but from a strong black *perspective.*"

The magazine had some unusual features. Not all models were slender beauties. Average-looking women modeled clothes that the readers could afford. As Marcia Ann Gillespie said, "Everybody's not a size 9, nor should she think she has to be."

The magazine didn't stick to easy, safe topics. It included subjects like politics, war, and religion. It often got its readers angry, but it was read. The editors and the publisher often disagreed, but out of disagreement came interesting subjects.

Essence has a popular letters column called "Write On." Here the readers did not hold back any punches. The criticism was helpful.

Susan Taylor first saw *Essence* way back in 1970. She had walked into a candy store to buy a magazine. When she looked over the familiar ones, she saw something new. It was *Essence.* It featured a black woman on the cover.

Susan Taylor became excited as she read it. As she said later, "I didn't know whether to read it or hug it."

When she was 25, Susan Taylor became fashion and beauty editor of *Essence*. That was in 1971. She dared to be different. She didn't believe in quick-weight-loss diets, for example. These were circulation builders in other magazines. Instead she featured weight control through good nutrition. She also provided career advice before other magazines took up the idea.

In 1981 Susan Taylor took over as head editor. She continued the excellent projects of earlier editors-in-chief. These projects included stories by major black writers. Among those who have appeared in *Essence* are Maya Angelou, Toni Cade Bambara, Amiri Baraka, Nikki Giovanni, June Jordan, Paule Marshall, Toni Morrison, Gloria Naylor, Larry Neal, Les Payne, Ishmael Reed, Ntozake Shange, and Alice Walker. Susan continues to encourage black writers to submit material.

She kept the good qualities and made some changes. She broadened the magazine's appeal to men. There is an annual issue on men and a monthly column by men. This column, "Say, Brother," is one of the most popular in the magazine.

Susan Taylor looks at men–women relationships in a special way. She feels that some problems of black men and women are brought on by society. She is frank, outspoken, honest. She encourages her writers to be the same. She challenges old ideas about the limited interests of black women.

Let's look at a typical table of contents. This will show how many subjects *Essence* covers. The fifteenth-anniversary issue, for example, contains the usual articles on health, diet, beauty, and fashion. But there is so much more.

There is Susan Taylor's own monthly column, "In the

Spirit." In it she appeals to black women for unity to gain political strength. An article by Dorothy Gilliam gives suggestions.

There's a tribute to Rosina Tucker, still active at age 103. There's also a tribute to Lena Horne. It tells her story, from poverty in Macon, Georgia, to success. Other courageous black women are praised, too.

In another article, Marcia Ann Gillespie, former editor-in-chief, interviews the writer Ntozake Shange. In 1976 Shange became an overnight success on Broadway. She frankly discusses the problems that success brought.

Frank and honest discussion is the *Essence* way. Susan Taylor has a goal. It is to make *Essence* more than entertainment. Since she is proud of her background, she hopes through the magazine to make all black women proud of their *heritage*. She insists that "black is beautiful," but she goes further. She looks at the whole world and its people.

One of the articles in *Essence* is titled "Sisterhood Is Global." *Essence* looks across the oceans. As Ed Lewis wrote, "This society—indeed, this world—is interdependent. Africa, for example, provides over 60% of our strategic minerals, including zinc, iron ore, and magnesium. We need them; they need us. And the same can be said for the remaining Third World countries and Europe."

Susan Taylor has a busy life. She is the mother of a teenage daughter. She somehow finds time to attend Fordham University. She says she "feels like a sister" to *Essence* readers. She is concerned not only about the problem of black women. She is concerned about the well-being of all human beings. We are all part of the same family.

UNDERSTANDING WHAT YOU HAVE READ

Finding Another Title

1. Another good title for this selection might be
   (a) Black Writers of America (b) How Magazines
   Have Changed (c) Susan Taylor and the Growth
   of *Essence* (d) Magazines and the Rise of Television.

Getting the Main Idea

2. Susan Taylor (a) changed her mind about *Essence*
   (b) disagreed with the publisher of *Essence* (c) was
   fashion and beauty editor of *Essence* (d) has guided
   Essence into new and interesting areas.

Finding Details

3. All the following sports are mentioned EXCEPT
   (a) ice hockey (b) jogging (c) football (d) golf.
4. *Discover* is a magazine devoted to (a) hunting and
   fishing (b) travel (c) science (d) news.
5. Magazines of the same type are (a) *Scientific
   American* and *Time* (b) *Ms.* and *U.S. News & World
   Report* (c) *Essence* and *Reader's Digest* (d) *Time*
   and *Newsweek*.
6. A magazine directed toward men is (a) *Newsweek*
   (b) *Field and Stream* (c) *Scientific American*
   (d) *Saturday Evening Post*.
7. The fifteenth anniversary of *Essence* appeared in
   (a) 1970 (b) 1971 (c) 1976 (d) 1985.

8. The first issue of *Essence* sold   (a) 50,000 copies   (b) 200,000 copies   (c) 800,000 copies   (d) four million copies.
9. Georgia Dullea is   (a) an editor   (b) a reporter   (c) a publisher   (d) a fashion model.
10. "In the Spirit" is written by   (a) Lena Horne   (b) Susan Taylor   (c) Marcia Ann Gillespie   (d) Ed Lewis.

Making Inferences

11. *Life* and the *Saturday Evening Post* can be classified as   (a) "special magazines"   (b) "science magazines"   (c) "old-time giants"   (d) "sports magazines."
12. If you were a scientist interested in a difficult scientific subject, you would most likely read   (a) *Reader's Digest*   (b) *Scientific American*   (c) *U.S. News & World Report*   (d) *Discover.*
13. The circulation of the fifteenth anniversary issue of *Essence* proved that   (a) good luck is still an important part of success   (b) the publishers did not make a mistake in 15 years   (c) the magazine gave its readers what they wanted   (d) the publishers made a wrong guess when they started the magazine.
14. A word that might be used to describe Susan Taylor is   (a) *courageous*   (b) *bashful*   (c) *cruel*   (d) *sad.*
15. The column "Say, Brother" was started to   (a) win men readers for *Essence*   (b) give the point of view of Susan Taylor   (c) provide a column for the publisher   (d) explain the aims of the magazine.

Predicting What Happens Next

16. After the fifteenth anniversary issue of *Essence,* Susan Taylor probably **(a)** began planning the twentieth anniversary issue **(b)** decided to appeal more to men than to women **(c)** returned to her job as fashion and beauty editor **(d)** continued to seek new ideas for the magazine.

Deciding on the Order of Events

17. The following events are scrambled. Arrange them in proper order, as they happened. Use letters only.
(a) Susan Taylor becomes fashion and beauty editor of *Essence.*
(b) Ntozake Shange has a hit on Broadway.
(c) *Essence* puts out its fifteenth anniversary issue.
(d) Susan Taylor sees her first copy of *Essence.*

Inferring Attitude

18. The attitude of the writer of the chapter toward Susan Taylor is one of **(a)** disapproval **(b)** surprise at her success **(c)** admiration **(d)** limited approval.

Separating Facts from Opinions

For each of the following, tell whether the statement is a fact (*F*) or an opinion (*O*).
19. The fifteenth anniversary issue of *Essence* was the best in its history.
20. Marcia Ann Gillespie was once editor-in-chief of *Essence.*

Understanding Words from Context

21. Your interests need not be active or *strenuous*.
    Strenuous (182) means   (a) dull   (b) lighthearted
    (c) harmful   (d) taking up energy.
22. Ed Lewis said, "We were terribly excited as we
    anticipated the birth of our first issue and had
    many questions."
    Anticipated (183) means   (a) looked forward to
    (b) worried about   (c) developed and planned
    (d) reported in detail.
23. Georgia Dullea wrote, "Fashion, beauty, food, health,
    child care, the usual women's magazine fare, was
    covered, but from a strong black *perspective*."
    Perspective (184) means   (a) biography   (b) point
    of view   (c) argument   (d) way of photographing.
24. Since she is proud of her background, she hopes
    through the magazine to make all black women proud
    of their *heritage*.
    Heritage (186) means   (a) financial assistance
    (b) money inherited from an uncle or an aunt
    (c) things we get from ancestors   (d) success in the
    modern world.
25. "Sisterhood is *global*"; our concerns are universal.
    Global (186) means   (a) rounded   (b) worldwide
    (c) necessary   (d) something desirable.

THINKING IT OVER

1. Why do you think general magazines have lost circulation while specialized magazines have gained
   circulation?

2. What is your favorite magazine? Tell why you like it.
3. How does a magazine differ from a newspaper?
4. What did Marcia Ann Gillespie mean when she said, "Everybody's not a size 9, nor should she think she has to be"? Do you agree? Explain.
5. Susan Taylor tried to draw male readers to her women's magazine. Do you think this was a good thing? Explain.
6. *Essence* says, "Sisterhood is global." Do you believe that we should be concerned about people in faraway countries, people we'll never meet? Explain.

ANOTHER LOOK AT THE QUOTATION

I would rather fail in an attempt at something new and uncharted than safely succeed in a repeat of something I have done.

A. E. HOTCHNER

1. Explain the quotation in your own words.
2. How did Susan Taylor introduce new ideas into magazine editing?
3. Do you like to explore new and different experiences, or do you prefer the familiar? Explain.

WORDS AT YOUR SERVICE—COMMON GREEK ROOTS

Some critics thought that *television* would kill most magazines. (182)

In the last chapter you learned a number of Latin roots. In this one you'll meet some roots that come to us from ancient Greek. These roots appear in many common words. The word *television* is an example.

Television contains the Greek root *tele,* meaning *distant, far off. Television* allows us to see things that are "distant." The *telegraph* allows us to write "at a distance," to send messages across distances. The *telephone* allows us to speak "at a distance." Sending data from a space ship to earth is called *telemetry.* This is truly measurement "at a distance." Some people believe that thoughts can be sent from one person to another "at a distance." This supposed ability is called *telepathy.* A *teletype* machine allows us to send printed messages "at a distance." *Telecommunications* are all communications "at a distance." They include cable, radio, telegraph, television, and telephone.

Do you see how a single root can be used over and over again for different words with a common idea?

Here are five additional Greek roots.

Root	*Meaning*	*Example*	*Definition of the English Word*
therm	heat	*therm*ostat	device for regulating *heat*
bio	life, living	*bio*graphy	story of a person's *life*
graph	write	auto*graph*	*written* by oneself
log	word, study	psycho*logy*	*study of* the mind
micro	small	*micro*be	*small* living creature

Fill in the blank in each sentence by supplying the missing root from the list on the previous page. The number in parentheses tells you how many letters you need. Use your dictionary to help you.

EXAMPLE

A ____scope allows us to see *at a distance*. (4)
Insert *tele*. The complete word is *telescope*.

1. A device that allows us to see very *small* things is a ____scope. (5)
2. The study of *living* things is called ____logy. (3)
3. The *written* story of a person's life is a bio____y. (5)
4. A device for measuring *heat* is a ____ometer. (5)
5. *Study of* the earth is called geo____y. (3)

COMPLETING AN OUTLINE

The article on Susan L. Taylor might be outlined in the following way. Five outline items have been omitted. Test your understanding of the structure of the article by following the directions after the outline.

   I. The modern newsstand
     A. Loss of old-time giant magazines
     B.

  II. A new magazine—*Essence*
     A.
     B. Readership—black women
     C. First sale—50,000

III. Problems and achievements
   A. Too much high fashion
   B. Exciting topics
   C.
   D. Black viewpoint

IV. Susan Taylor and the meeting with *Essence*
   A. First meeting—1970
   B.
   C. Introduction of new ideas

V. Susan Taylor—editor-in-chief
   A. Encouragement of black writers
   B. Appeal to men as well as women
   C.
   D. Preparation of fifteenth-anniversary issue
   E. Beliefs and goals

Fill in the items omitted from the outline. Correctly match the items in column A with the outline numbers in column B, which show where each item belongs in the outline.

A	B
1. Writing the column "In the Spirit"	**a.** I.B.
2. Average people as models	**b.** II.A.
3. First published in 1970	**c.** III.C.
4. Rise of specialized magazines	**d.** IV.B.
5. Appointment as fashion and beauty editor	**e.** V.C.

TWYLA THARP:

Artist of the Dance

*The truest expression of a people is in
its dances and its music.*

AGNES DE MILLE

"I was so happy I danced with joy."

This every-day saying tells us something about dancing. Dancing is a normal way to show emotion. It is a source of recreation and joy. It is not something discovered recently. It goes back to early times, to the days before records were kept.

Someone has compared the universe to a great ballet. The stars, the comets, and the planets all move in a rhythmic way, as in a dance. Our own bodies have their rhythms. Our breathing, our heart beat, our daily cycles all follow the order of the dance. Dancing comes naturally to us.

There was no written language when people first danced. We know about these dances from early paintings. A wonderful wall painting in Algeria shows masked dancers with arms outstretched and legs in a dance pattern. A rock painting shows a man hopping with lifted leg.

The history of Western dance begins in Egypt. An Egyptian vase painted 5,500 years ago shows a girl with arms over her head. She looks like a modern ballet dancer. This same gesture appears often in the art of other countries.

Dancing has always been connected with all kinds of emotion, even grief. In Egypt, the dance was an important part of funeral ceremonies. Dancers with slow, calm movements walked with the *solemn* procession to the tomb.

Dancers appear often in the art of nations other than Egypt. Pictures of the dances of Crete are very interesting. If we can judge by these pictures, Cretan dancers were freer than those of Egypt. As in Egypt, dancing played a role in the religious festivals. But in Crete the dancing was more athletic and exciting. Some pictures show women, probably priestesses, dancing with a snake in each hand. Other pictures show young men turning somersaults over the backs of bulls.

The Spartans of Greece used dancing as military exercises. The moves of the dance prepared young people for combat. One piece of wall sculpture shows warriors dancing in full battle dress.

Through the centuries dance has remained an important part of the life of the people. Different times and different areas of the world developed different dances. Often these dances showed the national character. The Virginia reel of nineteenth-century America *reflected* the lively energy of the frontier. By contrast, the stately minuet of seventeenth-century France showed the slower pace of court life.

Does dancing play a role in your life? Are you eager to learn the latest dance steps and dance with your friends? As you lose yourself in the music and the moves of the dance, you can appreciate the power of the dance.

Good dancers are fun to watch. Some people regularly attend dance performances, just as others go to the movies. Hollywood has often combined the appeal of both. The giant musicals of the 1930s depended on elaborate dances for their success. True geniuses like Fred Astaire made dancing almost as popular as baseball. In his 1952 movie *Singin' in the Rain,* Gene Kelly created a dance that often appears on television shows about dancing and about Hollywood.

The movies of recent years have kept the interest alive. John Travolta's *Saturday Night Fever,* in 1978, was a box-office smash hit. Then, in 1983, *Flashdance,* with Jennifer Beals, was another hit. Shortly after, *Footloose,* with Kevin Bacon, again successfully appealed to America's young people. TV music videos have further extended the appeal of dancing.

Many of our modern dances can trace their origins back hundreds of years. Jazz, breakdancing, and tap dancing, for example, have their roots in earlier forms of dance. Many folk dances like the Scottish Highland fling, the

Irish jig, and the English Morris dance, also trace their origins to an earlier day. Even children's games like "London Bridge" and "The Farmer in the Dell" are old folk dances.

Ballet also has its roots in past dances. It probably began before the sixteenth century. It has *retained* its hold for more than 400 years. Some of the world's greatest composers have provided music for the ballet. Tchaikovsky's *Sleeping Beauty* and *Nutcracker Suite* are still favorites.

Ballet always had a rather specialized appeal. Not everyone enjoyed it. Then in 1943 Agnes de Mille created dances for the American musical *Oklahoma*. These dance sequences helped many people to enjoy the ballet and made a lasting impression on the Broadway musical.

A person who creates dances is called a *choreographer*. Most choreographers are also skillful dancers. Agnes de Mille's experience as a dancer helped her develop skills as a choreographer.

Like Agnes de Mille, George Balanchine started as a dancer. He then became a choreographer, perhaps the greatest of modern times. Until his death in 1983, Balanchine ruled the ballet stage. In 1948 he became artistic director of the New York City Ballet and made it one of the world's outstanding ballet companies. His career extended over 60 years. His productions are an honor roll of ballet. Few choreographers have shown the depth and genius of George Balanchine.

Who is the successor to Balanchine? Some people think it is Twyla Tharp. She is small and delicately featured. Her slight frame hides her strength. She is a bundle of energy and a creative genius. As time goes on, she dances less and less. But she pours all her energy into creating new dances. Twyla Tharp has combined careers as a dancer and choreographer. She has experimented with both modern dance and ballet.

Twyla Tharp developed her skills early. She was born on July 1, 1941, in Portland, Indiana. Her mother, a pianist, gave Twyla piano lessons when Twyla was two and dancing lessons by the time she was four. Her dancing lessons included tap dancing, ballet, and baton twirling.

Her music education was not *skimpy,* either. She learned to play the violin and the viola. She studied music theory, harmony, and composition. Though she originally intended to be a doctor, she shifted her course to art history.

When she was in college, she studied classic ballet at the American Ballet Theater School. Classic ballet holds to the forms and steps of the past. She did not neglect other forms of dance. She studied modern dance at the studio of the great dancer Martha Graham. She learned jazz dancing as well.

After college she joined the Paul Taylor Dance Company and became a leading dancer. Although she stayed with the group only about a year, she learned a great deal. She left the group in 1965 and was soon creating dances for her own company of four female dancers, including herself. Her first year on her own was busy.

She has experimented with all kinds of dances in all kinds of settings. She presented a new dance at the Judson Memorial Church in Greenwich Village, in New York City. Another of her dances was planned to be performed on a basketball court. Still another was performed in the open air in Central Park. Oddly enough, most of Twyla Tharp's early works were designed to be performed on a bare stage, without scenery or music.

Then came a period of rapid growth. Twyla and her company accepted a number of short-term assignments at colleges and universities. Some of her dances of this period were made for college campuses.

In 1971 Twyla presented *Eight Jelly Rolls.* This dance was set to the jazz music of Jelly Roll Morton. Dance critic Marcia B. Siegel said that this dance "is built for the audience." With it Twyla won the hearts of many people who had formerly laughed at the dance. Dance critic John Rockwell called Twyla Tharp "an artist who could bridge the seemingly *contradictory* worlds of modern dance experimentation, pop, and ballet."

Twyla Tharp uses her own dance company to invent new dances. She once said, "Working with my own dancers allows me to make discoveries and advances. Artists must be allowed to *wallow* around in their own confusion, and that can lead to other, more finished things."

Twyla has worked on so many different kinds of dances that she is hard to pin down. But most critics consider her a genius in classical ballet. *Bach Partita* is already recognized as one of the great works of the ballet theater. The American Ballet Theater performs it regularly. Audiences come back again and again to see this masterpiece as it is danced by six superb dancers.

Twyla Tharp creates dances for special occasions and for special friends. For the great dancer Baryshnikov she created *Sinatra Suite*. She created the dances for the movie *Amadeus*. Her restless eye is everywhere, seeking ideas to use. Writers put their ideas into words. She puts hers into the dance.

Twyla Tharp continues to take on new roles, to move in new directions. In 1985 she directed the Broadway stage version of the movie *Singin' in the Rain*. Of her work, Twyla said, "Getting performances out of people is extremely creative and, in the long run, that's what directing is about. It doesn't matter whether you're creating a dance for the first time, or working with old material. It's up to you to make it work."

Twyla Tharp's future is bright. Another choreographer, Sophie Maslow, once said, "A dancer has to stop. . . . There is a limit for the body. But a choreographer can continue to choreograph, just as a writer can continue to write."

The ballet is expanding. Ballet companies have formed everywhere. There are ballet companies in Boston, Cincinnati, Philadelphia, Salt Lake City, and many other cities. You can be sure that many companies throughout the world put on the dances of Twyla Tharp.

UNDERSTANDING WHAT YOU HAVE READ

Finding Another Title

1. Another good title for this selection might be (a) The Dance: from Ancient Times to Twyla Tharp (b) The Link Between Religion and the Dance (c) How Movies Use Dances for Greater Audience Appeal (d) George Balanchine: Master of the Modern Dance.

Getting the Main Idea

2. Twyla Tharp (a) is a cautious person who worries about new projects (b) was selected by George Balanchine to carry on his work (c) has limited her work to the classical ballet (d) has created new and original dances of many types.

Finding Details

3. Dancing was used as a military exercise by the (a) Spartans (b) Cretans (c) Egyptians (d) Algerians.
4. The Virginia reel is a dance of (a) the American cities (b) the frontier (c) highly skilled dancers (d) the Blue Ridge Mountains.
5. The music for *The Sleeping Beauty* was created by (a) George Balanchine (b) Agnes de Mille (c) Tchaikovsky (d) Baryshnikov.
6. Martha Graham is mentioned as a (a) member of Twyla Tharp's company (b) dance critic (c) dance partner of John Travolta (d) great dancer.
7. Twyla Tharp is like Paul Taylor in that they (a) were born in the same year (b) studied under Balanchine (c) were directors of the American Ballet Theater (d) both had their own dance companies.
8. *Eight Jelly Rolls* was first presented in (a) 1941 (b) 1961 (c) 1971 (d) 1983.
9. A classical ballet created by Twyla Tharp is (a) *Sinatra Suite* (b) *Flashdance* (c) *Bach Partita* (d) *Saturday Night Fever*.
10. *Amadeus* is mentioned as a (a) ballet (b) movie (c) folk dance (d) television special.

Making Inferences

11. The selection suggests that dancing is a good way to (a) express feelings (b) make new friends (c) waste time (d) show off.
12. We may assume that dancing (a) is always joyous (b) helps reflect different moods (c) makes a great deal of money for all dancers (d) is not found in tribes of today.

13. The Spartans were most likely (a) the best dancers of ancient times (b) opposed to all forms of dancing (c) a military society (d) the creators of the English Morris dance.

14. A good choreographer (a) has usually been a dancer (b) does not accept the suggestions of others (c) creates only ballets (d) will not work for the movies.

15. Twyla Tharp might not have been so successful (a) if she had not met Agnes de Mille (b) without the early training provided by her mother (c) if she had not created the dances for *Saturday Night Fever* (d) if she had met Balanchine earlier.

Predicting What Happens Next

16. After her success with *Bach Partita*, Twyla Tharp most likely (a) asked Baryshnikov to dance in it (b) refused to do another classical ballet (c) got bored with it and never had it produced again (d) kept experimenting with all kinds of dances.

Deciding on the Order of Events

17. The following events are scrambled. Arrange them in proper order, as they happened. Use letters only.
    (a) Agnes de Mille creates dances for *Oklahoma*.
    (b) George Balanchine dies.
    (c) Twyla Tharp presents *Eight Jelly Rolls*.
    (d) Twyla Tharp leaves the Paul Taylor Dance Company.

Inferring Tone

18. In talking of her use of the dance company (200), Twyla Tharp is **(a)** hopeful **(b)** downhearted **(c)** bored **(d)** angry.

Separating Facts from Opinions

For each of the following, tell whether the statement is a fact (*F*) or an opinion (*O*).
19. Twyla Tharp's success was richly deserved.
20. Balanchine was the greatest ballet director of modern times.

Understanding Words from Context

21. Dancers with slow, calm movements walked with the *solemn* procession to the tomb.
    Solemn (196) means **(a)** happy **(b)** serious **(c)** unexpected **(d)** rehearsed.
22. Ballet probably began before the sixteenth century. It has *retained* its hold for more than 400 years.
    Retained (198) means **(a)** loosened **(b)** expanded **(c)** kept **(d)** advertised.
23. Her music education was not *skimpy,* either. She learned to play the violin and the viola.
    Skimpy (199) means **(a)** loud **(b)** rich **(c)** unprepared **(d)** incomplete.

24. Rockwell called Tharp "an artist who could bridge the seemingly *contradictory* worlds of modern dance experimentation, pop, and ballet."
    Contradictory (200) means (a) opposed (b) lively (c) difficult (d) musical.
25. Artists must be allowed to *wallow* around in their own confusion, to move about as they feel.
    Wallow (200) means (a) run (b) roll (c) complain (d) swallow.

THINKING IT OVER

1. Why do you think dance is so natural an activity for human beings?
2. How does a particular dance tell us something about the people who dance it?
3. Which kinds of modern dancing appeal most to you? Why?
4. Dance has been called a great source of relaxation. Do you agree? Explain.
5. Have you ever seen a ballet? If so, tell about it.
6. Twyla Tharp has worked in all kinds of dances. Why is this experience valuable in creating ballets?
7. Have you ever been square dancing or folk dancing? Did you enjoy it? Tell about it.
8. Do you enjoy a movie with lots of dancing? Explain.
9. Do you enjoy the dancing in music videos? Which video is your favorite?
10. Is it important for a popular singer to be able to dance reasonably well? Explain.

ANOTHER LOOK AT THE QUOTATION

*The truest expression of a people is in its
dances and its music.*

AGNES DE MILLE

1. Do you agree that dances and music express the
    attitudes of a people or a nation? Explain.
2. What other forms of creativity express the attitudes
    of a nation?
3. Would Twyla Tharp probably agree with Agnes de
    Mille? Why or why not?

WORDS AT YOUR SERVICE—PREFIXES

The Virginia reel of nineteenth-century America
reflected the lively energy of the frontier. (197)

In an earlier chapter you learned about prefixes, roots,
and suffixes. This chapter concentrates on prefixes. In the
sentence quoted above, *reflected* has a prefix, *re.* If you
know the prefix *re,* you have a key to the word *reflected*
and to dozens of others. *Re* means *back* or *again.* Note
how this information helps you remember the meanings
of many words.

remit—send back	*rebuild*—build again
repel—drive back	*reborn*—born again
report—carry back	*recapture*—capture again
refer—direct back	*recycle*—cycle, or use, again
reflect—shine back	*replace*—place again
reverse—turn back	*reset*—set again
rebound—bound back	*retry*—try again

Here are five additional helpful prefixes.

Prefix	Meaning of the Prefix	Example	Definition of the Word
anti	against, opposed	*anti*dote	medicine *against* poison
extra	beyond, outside	*extra*ordinary	*beyond* the ordinary
multi	many	*multi*ply	increase (make *many*)
pre	before	*pre*cede	go *before*
semi	half	*semi*circle	*half* a circle

Fill in the blank in each sentence by supplying the missing prefix from the list on the previous page. The number in parentheses tells you how many letters you need.

EXAMPLE

Mrs. Rodriguez is _____ novating her apartment with all *new* furniture. (2)
Insert *re*. The complete word is *renovating*.

1. A _____tude is made up of *many* people. (5)
2. The _____face of a book is placed *before* the main text. (3)
3. Mom put _____freeze in the car radiator to protect it *against* the cold weather. (4)
4. _____vagant people spend money *beyond* their means. (5)
5. Dues are collected _____annually, every *half* year, in January and July. (4)

LEWIS THOMAS:
Scientist and Writer

The larger the island of knowledge, the longer the shoreline of wonder.

RALPH W. SOCKMAN

As we become smarter, we realize how much we do not know. The march of science illustrates this point. Science is always turning up new facts about the world we live in. Each new find opens the door wider to the mysterious universe, our home.

Here's an example. Scientists had believed that life on other planets could not exist without water. They also thought life needed something like the moderate temperatures of our own planet. Yet here on Earth, some forms of life exist under "impossible" conditions. Bacteria live where life should not be able to survive.

Deep in the ocean there are splits in the Earth's crust. Through these splits, sea water pours forth at temperatures of 662 degrees or higher. Because of the great pressure, the water stays liquid. At 662 degrees the book you are holding would ignite and burn up. Surely nothing could live at a temperature that would burn paper? But something does.

Scientists scooped up some of this very hot water. The samples contained healthy groups of bacteria. These living organisms answer the question, "Can life survive under conditions of extreme heat?" But the answer, like many scientific answers, suggests more questions. "What special qualities do these bacteria have?" "What kind of protein can withstand the extreme heat?" "How does the *genetic* material—the material that allows us to pass on traits to our offspring—keep from melting?" "How could we reproduce these qualities?"

In an article, scientist Lewis Thomas talked about these "impossibilities." He is delighted and amazed with discoveries like this. He likes to help others get excited by science. As he wrote, "Nothing is the way we thought it was, and whatever we think we understand today will be changed to something else when looked at more closely tomorrow."

Thomas feels a sense of wonder about these discoveries. In addition, he is impressed by something else. In the book *The Medusa and the Snail,* he wrote, "Everything here is alive thanks to the living of everything else. All the forms of life are connected." He pays tribute to the lowliest forms of life. "Without bacteria for starters, we would never have had enough oxygen to go around . . . nor could we recycle the solid matter of life for new generations."

That we are here on Earth is a miracle. That we can survive on Earth depends on *untold* tiny and large creatures that work for us. Our survival depends on growing things, on the cooperation of the animal and the plant kingdoms. We owe our very lives to the most seemingly *unimportant* creatures.

We also owe our lives to each other. Thomas emphasizes our need to feel part of a group. We are members of a social group. We need to be in touch with others, to talk with them. We can be proud of our independence. But that independence is limited. For our very survival we depend on a network of people. So all life is connected.

Thomas often looks at the world upside down. Some writers seem to think we should be perfect. Thomas has another idea. He sees that mistakes play an important role in our lives. He says, "Mistakes are at the very base of human thought. . . . If we were not provided with the *knack* of being wrong, we could never get anything useful done. We think our way along by choosing between right and wrong alternatives, and the wrong choices have to be made as frequently as the right ones. We get along in life this way. We are built to make mistakes.

"We learn, as we say, by 'trial and error.' Why do we always say that? Why not 'trial and rightness' or 'trial and triumph'? The old phrase puts it that way because that is, in real life, the way it is done."

Thomas knows the great value of medical research. "Compared with a century ago, when every family was obliged to count on losing members throughout the early years of life, we are in a new world. A death in a young family has become a rare and dreadful *catastrophe,* no longer a commonplace event."

Oddly enough, these improvements have sometimes made us feel less safe. He feels that Americans may worry too much about health. The body is an amazing machine. As he says, "We are, in real life, a reasonably healthy people. Far from being ineptly put together, we are amazingly tough, *durable* organisms, full of health. . . . The new danger to our well-being, if we continue to listen to all the talk, is worrying ourselves half to death."

In an earlier book, *The Lives of a Cell,* he deals with a similar question. In a healthy person, "the great thing is that most things get better by themselves. Most things, in fact, are better by morning."

The body is a mysterious and complicated unit. The more we learn about it, the more awed we are. Thomas tells of a change in thinking. Two hundred years ago, scientists felt that eventually nature would reveal all its secrets. Great advances *were* made—in all areas of science. A fairly complete understanding of life seemed to lie just around the corner. Yet today Thomas says, "The only solid piece of scientific truth about which I feel totally confident is that we are profoundly ignorant about nature. Indeed, I regard this as the major discovery of the past hundred years of biology."

These ideas are just a sample of Thomas's interesting point of view. What kind of person is this scientist–writer? How did he get that way?

Lewis Thomas was born in 1913, the fourth of five children. His father was chief of surgery at Flushing Hospital in New York. Lewis Thomas got his bachelor's degree from

Princeton University in 1933. He earned his medical degree from the Harvard Medical School in 1937. He was an intern at the Boston City Hospital for two years, from 1937 to 1939.

Then he became a resident physician at a New York hospital. At first he seemed headed toward a career as a practicing doctor. But he was far more interested in uncovering new knowledge.

In 1941 he became a lieutenant in the United States Naval Reserve. He took a research post at the Rockefeller Institute. There he was assigned to the Naval Medical Research Unit. He carried out investigations on infectious diseases. In 1944 and 1945 he was sent to Guam and Okinawa to do research. He rose in the ranks and was discharged as a lieutenant commander in 1946. For the next eight years he held a variety of posts at various hospitals and universities. All were related to medical research.

For the next 12 years, Thomas worked at Bellevue Hospital in New York. He had a number of different jobs. Each experience sharpened his interest in scientific discovery. He was both teacher and researcher. During this period he and Dr. Benjamin Zweifach, a partner in research, made two startling discoveries.

In the first experiment, they injected rats with small amounts of a certain poison. These injections actually increased the resistance of the rats to poisons and burns. In the second experiment, they used rabbits to show how animals resist disease or injury.

Then came a great many assignments, too numerous to list here. Thomas became dean of the New York University School of Medicine. He worked with New York City on problems of drug addiction. He served as a member of the Board of Health.

He found the duties of administration too boring after

a while, though. In 1969 he became a professor at Yale University. In 1972 he acted as chairman of the National Academy of Sciences. In 1973 he became president of the Memorial Sloan-Kettering Cancer Center in New York City.

Throughout this busy period, Thomas found time to wonder . . . and to write. He wrote for many different magazines. One of his series of articles was called "Notes of a Biology Watcher." Soon 29 of these essays were collected into a book. *The Lives of a Cell* made Thomas famous. This book won the National Book Award in 1974. A reviewer for *Newsweek* called Thomas "one of the best writers of the short essay in English."

In *The Medusa and the Snail,* Thomas continued his favorite subjects. He showed again and again how living creatures depend on other living creatures. The title of the book suggests these relationships. The medusa, a kind of jellyfish, cannot exist without a particular snail. The snail cannot exist without the medusa. As he wrote, "They depend for their survival on each other."

And so do we all.

UNDERSTANDING WHAT YOU HAVE READ

Finding Another Title

1. Another good title for this selection might be **(a)** An Interesting Life **(b)** Surprising Facts About Bacteria **(c)** Lewis Thomas and the Wonder of Life **(d)** Mysteries of the Human Body.

Getting the Main Idea

2. Which of the following best expresses the main idea of the selection?
   (a) In science every advance in knowledge shows how much we still have to learn.
   (b) Some creatures can live under conditions that seem impossible.
   (c) Lewis Thomas did a great deal of traveling.
   (d) Americans worry too much about their health.

Finding Details

3. The "amazing machine" that Thomas refers to is **(a)** a new X-ray **(b)** a device for getting oxygen from water **(c)** the human body **(d)** the medusa.
4. The two colleges where Thomas earned degrees were **(a)** Princeton and Harvard **(b)** Flushing and Harvard **(c)** Princeton and New York University **(d)** Flushing and Princeton.
5. Thomas had an assignment at the Rockefeller Institute in **(a)** 1937 **(b)** 1939 **(c)** 1941 **(d)** 1945.
6. The total number of years Thomas spent at Bellevue Hospital was **(a)** five **(b)** eight **(c)** ten **(d)** 12.

7. Dr. Benjamin Zweifach (a) worked with Thomas (b) was the real author of *The Medusa and the Snail* (c) was a lieutenant commander in the U.S. Navy (d) was chief of surgery at Flushing Hospital.
8. To study how animals resist disease, Thomas used (a) monkeys (b) rabbits (c) pigs (d) mice.
9. Thomas worked on problems of drug addiction in (a) Guam (b) Okinawa (c) Boston (d) New York.
10. The national magazine that paid tribute to Thomas was (a) *Time* (b) *Medical News* (c) *Newsweek* (d) *Scientific American.*

Making Inferences

11. Quotation marks are put around the word *impossible* on page 209 because (a) *impossible* here means *possible* (b) bacteria should not live when temperatures go above the boiling point of water (c) the author is quoting from Ralph Sockman (d) the author doesn't believe the reports about the bacteria.
12. When Thomas thinks of how much there is to be learned, he becomes (a) angry (b) sad (c) joyful (d) irritated.
13. One of Thomas's deepest beliefs is that (a) some day we will solve all problems in science (b) we should keep an open mind (c) Americans are not healthy (d) life is too short to take seriously.
14. When Lewis Thomas thinks about the health of human beings, he is (a) cheerful and hopeful (b) worried and anxious (c) fearful but brave (d) uninterested.
15. Lewis Thomas's experiences have been (a) limited (b) boring (c) varied (d) envied.

Predicting What Happens Next

16. After the scientists discovered living bacteria on the ocean's floor, they most likely **(a)** kept the discovery secret for a year   **(b)** kept exploring for new life   **(c)** gave up further exploration   **(d)** called Lewis Thomas on the ship's telephone.

Deciding on the Order of Events

17. The following events are scrambled. Arrange them in proper order, as they happened. Use letters only.
    (a) Thomas becomes president of the Memorial Sloan-Kettering Cancer Center.
    (b) *The Lives of a Cell* wins the National Book Award.
    (c) Thomas becomes dean of the New York University School of Medicine.
    (d) Thomas is an intern at the Boston City Hospital.

Inferring Tone

18. The tone, or attitude, of the quotation about bacteria and their role in life (210) is one of   **(a)** self-satisfaction   **(b)** wonder   **(c)** annoyance   **(d)** lighthearted humor.

Separating Facts from Opinions

For each of the following, tell whether the statement is a fact (*F*) or an opinion (*O*).

19. The discovery of bacteria living at 662 degrees is amazing.
20. *The Lives of a Cell* and *The Medusa and the Snail* are equally good.

Understanding Words from Context

21. How does the *genetic* material—the material that
allows us to pass on traits to our offspring—keep
from melting?
Genetic (209) has to do with (a) heat and cold
(b) moisture (c) inherited qualities (d) size and
shape.
22. That we can survive on Earth depends on *untold*
tiny and large creatures that work for us.
Untold (210) means (a) unwilling to speak (b)
unwelcome (c) unexpected (d) too many to count.
23. Thomas says, "If we were not provided with the
knack of being wrong, we could never get anything
useful done."
Knack (210) means (a) foolishness (b) skill
(c) effort (d) weariness.
24. Thomas says, "A death in a young family has become
a rare and dreadful *catastrophe,* no longer a commonplace event."
Catastrophe (211) means (a) situation (b) news
report (c) relaxation (d) disaster.
25. Thomas says, "We are amazingly tough, *durable*
organisms."
Durable (211) means (a) lasting (b) friendly
(c) fragile (d) clever.

THINKING IT OVER

1. Have you ever learned by trial and error? Tell about
your experience.
2. Is it possible to worry too much about health? Give
examples to prove your point.

3. Some people think we should spend a great deal of money on space travel. Exploring space would help us gain new knowledge. Others think we should give up the space program and concentrate on improving conditions here on Earth. Still others try to compromise. Tell how you feel.
4. Do you agree with Lewis Thomas that every living thing depends on all other living things? Explain.
5. "If you want to get a job done, give it to a busy person." What does this saying mean? Did Lewis Thomas prove this advice to be true?

ANOTHER LOOK AT THE QUOTATION

The larger the island of knowledge,
the longer the shoreline of wonder.
RALPH W. SOCKMAN

1. Explain the quotation in your own words.
2. Would Lewis Thomas be likely to agree with Ralph W. Sockman? Why or why not?
3. Do you ever find yourself wondering about life on Earth, about the stars, about the future of people on Earth? Tell about your daydreams.
4. Some modern scientific discoveries are stranger than science fiction. What is the most amazing discovery you have read about? Why was this discovery so astounding? What was the most amazing science-fiction movie you have seen? Did you enjoy it? Why or why not?
5. Is a sense of wonder good for a scientist? Explain.

WORDS AT YOUR SERVICE—PREFIXES FOR *NOT*

> We owe our very lives to the most seemingly *unimportant* creatures. (210)
> Yet here on Earth, some forms of life exist under *"impossible"* conditions. (209)

The words *unimportant* and *impossible* contain two of the most helpful prefixes in English: *un* and *im*. Both mean *not* in the sentences quoted. *Un* is one of the most reliable of all prefixes. You find it in *unattractive, unbeaten, unchanged, unconscious, undecided, unemployed, uneven, unhappy, unhealthy, uninterrupted, unjust,* and dozens of other words. In all these words *un* means *not*.

The prefix *im* meaning *not* has several spellings.

> ig - ignorant - not knowing
> il - illegal - not legal
> im - impersonal - not personal
> in - independent - not dependent
> ir - irresponsible - not responsible

When you see a new word beginning with one of the *im* prefixes, be careful. In some words, like *important,* the prefix does not mean *not*. Still, *im* is a useful prefix to know.

ROBERT H. GODDARD:

Rocket Pioneer

*If you want something very badly, you
can achieve it. It may take patience, very
hard work, a real struggle, and a long
time; but it can be done.*

MARGO JONES

"The man must be crazy! He says a rocket could fly to the moon. It could somehow travel through the vacuum of outer space under its own power. That's a stupid idea. It can't be done. Goddard is a hopeless dreamer. He's moon-mad."

Many people expressed thoughts like these in 1920. Even the *New York Times* poked fun at Robert H. Goddard's claim that a rocket could reach the moon. But on July 17, 1969, the *Times* printed a formal apology for its negative comments of 49 years earlier. What happened that had changed people's views? On that date the *Apollo XI* astronauts were circling the moon and getting ready for a landing! Goddard's dream had come true.

Who was this man who foresaw the moon landing half a century before it occurred? Robert H. Goddard was born in 1882, before humans made flights of any kind. But he dreamed of flight. He became fascinated by rockets at an early age and thought they might be useful for space travel. Few people agreed with this idea.

Rockets had been known for many years. A thousand years ago the Chinese used the rockets for weapons and for religious purposes. In the thirteenth century, the English monk Roger Bacon experimented with rockets.

During the War of 1812, the British used rockets against Fort McHenry. These are mentioned in "The Star-Spangled Banner"—"the rockets' red glare."

Through the centuries rockets have been used with varying success. Goddard did not invent the rocket, but he saw uses others had failed to see.

How could a rocket travel? People believed that a rocket got its *thrust* from pushing against the atmosphere. In the vacuum of outer space, there would be nothing to push against. People thought a rocket would not work there.

The opposite is true. A rocket works best in a vacuum. It carries chemicals that *enable* it to burn its fuel without taking air from outside. It is perfectly self-contained. The emptiness of outer space provides easy highways for rockets to fly in. Modern jet-propelled aircraft use the reaction force of rockets, but there is a difference. Jet engines use outside air. Rockets do not.

Most people of Goddard's time thought that rockets were little more than toys. They made good fireworks. Goddard saw rockets as vital to the future.

Even as a boy, Goddard experimented with rockets. Once he was kept in his room because of sickness. He prepared a demonstration. He took a curtain rod from the bedroom window and the pendulum from the clock. He added other materials. For safety he put a blanket on the ceiling. He invited his family in to watch.

Goddard set off the rocket. Off it went—but not toward the protected ceiling. It headed straight for the closed window. The broken window provided a lesson. Goddard had many failures in his long career with rockets, but he learned from every one.

Goddard was interested in space travel. As a child he read H. G. Wells's *War of the Worlds*. In this novel, invaders from Mars come to Earth and almost take over the planet. He read scientific magazines. He majored in physics at Clark University in Worcester, Massachusetts.

At the university he began studying possible rocket fuels. He decided that a combination of liquid hydrogen and liquid oxygen would be the best fuels. Neither fuel was then available for sale.

In 1916 Goddard was given a grant of $5,000 by the Smithsonian Institution to build test rockets. As a result of his experiments, he published an important paper. This study contained his ideas on sending rockets to great heights. In it he mentioned the possibility of using rockets to reach the moon. Although his ideas were sound, the public attacked his thoughts about reaching the moon. Goddard was thought to be a hopeless dreamer.

A pioneer faces many difficulties. People laughed at Goddard. But he faced practical problems as well as *ridicule*. His tests were noisy. In 1929 a particularly loud flight frightened the neighbors. Ambulances, police, and reporters came rushing to his Aunt Effie's farm, where he was carrying out the tests. Goddard had to move his testing to another area—the artillery range at Fort Devens.

Few people had faith in Goddard, and his spirits must have fallen. Then later in 1929 a famous American stepped in to help.

Colonel Charles Lindbergh had made the famous solo flight from New York to Paris in 1927. Lindbergh was impressed by Goddard's work. He was also convinced that rocketry had a bright future. Through Lindbergh's help, Goddard received a grant of $50,000 from Daniel Guggenheim.

Testing rockets was expensive. Goddard at last had enough funds. He headed to Roswell, New Mexico. Here both climate and setting were perfect for his experiments. He made his headquarters at a place called Eden Valley. He set up a busy schedule. For the next ten years he carried out a test every three weeks.

His staff at Eden Valley was never large. Seven was the usual number. There were five who created the rockets, a photographer, and a person who put out any rocket fires. The rockets were made to order. Goddard bought materials from large mail-order houses. His crew prowled through stores looking for usable parts. They checked hardware stores, sporting-goods stores, and auto-parts stores.

They used materials in unexpected ways. A child's wristwatch, a length of piano wire, or a spark plug might come in handy. The staff used rocket parts over and over again. Many rockets returned to Earth with a crash and were *converted* to *useless* junk. Couldn't these parts be saved? Goddard designed a rocket-recovery system using parachutes for softer landings.

Many of the early space flights used parachutes to land space capsules more gently. But Goddard had the idea first.

Goddard was first in so many ways. As early as 1914 he invented a two-stage rocket. He was the first to use the idea of stages. This is a commonplace idea today. In March 1926 Goddard completed and fired the world's first liquid-fuel rocket.

He continued to invent. His *ingenious* mind went on and on, continually working on new ideas. In 1929 he fired the first rocket to contain an instrument package. It carried a barometer, a thermometer, and a camera. To keep his rockets on course, he experimented with guidance systems. He invented the first practical automatic steering device for rockets. He developed the first smokeless powder rocket. He was granted more than 200 patents on his inventions.

Goddard wasn't entirely happy with the progress of rocketry, though. He was worried about certain possibilities. He realized that the new rockets could be used for military purposes. He was afraid that Germany might be planning to use deadly rockets in war. He was right, but nobody listened.

In 1939, the year World War II began, thousands of Germans were at work on a rocket project. Their efforts brought forth the V-2 rockets in 1942. These rockets struck terrible blows at the British Isles toward the end of the war. When these rockets were captured and shown to Goddard, he gasped. Goddard and his small crew at Roswell had built and flown rockets like these three years before!

The first episode of the TV mini-series *Space* told this story. It showed how much damage the German rockets had done. It described Allied efforts to cripple the rocket bases. At this time the rest of the world was far behind the Germans. The Germans themselves were amazed that the U.S. government had shown no interest in rockets like the V-2. Wernher von Braun, the German rocket expert, declared in 1950, "Goddard was ahead of us all."

The government did call Goddard into service during the war. He worked on rocket-assisted take-off for regular aircraft. Goddard did not, however, live to see the end of the war. He died in Baltimore on August 10, 1945, four days before the surrender of Japan.

In the Space Age, Goddard's achievements are becoming more and more evident. He was not entirely alone in his glimpse of the future. Like Goddard, Konstantin Tsiolkovsky, from Russia, and Hermann Oberth, from Germany, worked out early calculations on rocketry and space flight. But Goddard took these ideas further and tried them out. He designed machinery and equipment. He worked on fuels. He built rockets and actually flew them. He put his theories to practical tests.

Humans have walked on the moon. Spacecraft have landed on Venus and Mars. *Voyager 1* and *Voyager 2* have taken remarkable pictures of Saturn, Jupiter, and their many satellites. That is only the beginning of the story.

On March 3, 1972, *Pioneer 10* took off for a look at Jupiter. On December 3, 1973, it gave the first close-up view of that planet. It continued on its swing through the solar system. Thirteen years later, in 1986, it became the first human-made object to leave the solar system behind and head into deep space! We have finally reached for the stars.

One man played a major role in the development of all these space marvels. Rocket expert Jerome Hunsaker has said, "Every liquid-fuel rocket that flies is a Goddard rocket."

In 1962 the National Aeronautics and Space Administration's research area at Greenbelt, Maryland, was named the *Goddard Space Flight Center.* This was an honor richly deserved.

UNDERSTANDING WHAT YOU HAVE READ

Finding Another Title

1. Another good title for this selection might be (a) Rockets and War Strategy (b) How Rockets Took Us to the Moon (c) Successes and Disappointments (d) The Man Who Helped Make Space Travel Possible.

Getting the Main Idea

2. Robert H. Goddard (a) kept true to his lifelong dream (b) was a good friend of Charles Lindbergh (c) was an encouraging leader (d) hoped one day to fly to the moon.

Finding Details

3. Goddard was once made fun of by (a) *Time* magazine (b) the *New York Times* (c) *Aviation Week* (d) *Modern Times.*

4. The *Apollo* flight that first landed on the moon was numbered (a) IX (b) X (c) XI (d) XII.
5. When Goddard was born, (a) rockets had not yet been invented (b) rockets had reached a height of five miles in the air (c) no human had made a power-driven flight (d) the U.S. Army was already interested in rockets.
6. Goddard was influenced by a book written by (a) Wernher von Braun (b) Charles Lindbergh (c) H. G. Wells (d) Roger Bacon.
7. Charles Lindbergh was most famous for his (a) support of Robert Goddard (b) airplane flight to Paris (c) heroic deeds in World War II (d) work on rockets.
8. Goddard completed the first liquid-fuel rocket in (a) 1914 (b) 1926 (c) 1929 (d) 1941.
9. The land most hurt by the V-2 rockets was (a) France (b) Germany (c) the United States (d) the British Isles.
10. Konstantin Tsiolkovsky came from (a) Russia (b) Germany (c) Baltimore (d) the British Isles.

Making Inferences

11. Goddard was called *moon-mad* because he (a) was an outstanding astronomer (b) believed people would reach the moon some day (c) wrote a science-fiction novel about the moon (d) thought the moon affected our everyday behavior.
12. Before Goddard showed the way, people's belief about the thrust of a rocket in outer space was (a) wrong (b) never actually stated (c) the basis of early space flights (d) correct, but incomplete.

13. Good words to describe Goddard's staff at Eden Valley are (a) *clever* and *inventive* (b) *intelligent* but *easily discouraged* (c) *enthusiastic* but *careless* (d) *tense* and *unhappy*.

14. Wernher von Braun (a) admired the U.S. government's work on rockets (b) worked on rockets for England (c) thought that Goddard was not appreciated by his own government (d) was the inventor of the two-stage rocket.

15. If Goddard had been taken more seriously in his early years, (a) he most likely would have soon lost interest in rockets (b) jet aircraft would not have been invented (c) he would have been elected to Congress (d) space travel probably would have developed sooner.

Predicting What Happens Next

16. The U.S. government will most likely (a) give up the space program (b) continue to develop rockets along the lines suggested by Goddard (c) change the name of Kennedy Space Center to *Goddard Space Center* (d) express regret that Goddard had not been honored in his early years.

Deciding on the Order of Events

17. The following events are scrambled. Arrange them in order, as they happened. Use letters only.
    (a) Charles Lindbergh helps Robert Goddard.
    (b) Goddard dies in Baltimore.
    (c) An astronaut walks on the moon.
    (d) Goddard is given a grant by the Smithsonian Institution.

Inferring Tone

18. The opinions about Goddard expressed in the opening paragraph (221) can best be described as
(a) flattering **(b)** encouraging **(c)** insulting
(d) uncertain.

Separating Facts from Opinions

For each of the following, tell whether the statement is a fact (*F*) or an opinion (*O*).
19. Goddard predicted moon travel many years before the first landing on the moon.
20. The U.S. government was foolish in not putting Goddard to work on rockets like the V-2.

Understanding Words from Context

21. How could a rocket travel? People believed that a rocket got its *thrust* from pushing against the atmosphere.
Thrust (221) means **(a)** ignition **(b)** weight
(c) push **(d)** distance.
22. The rocket carries chemicals that *enable* it to burn its fuel without taking air from outside.
Enable (221) means **(a)** allow **(b)** prevent
(c) encourage **(d)** tell.

23. People laughed at Goddard. But he faced practical problems as well as *ridicule*.
Ridicule (223) means **(a)** advice **(b)** failure **(c)** anger **(d)** scorn.

24. Many rockets returned to Earth with a crash and were *converted* to useless junk.
Converted (223) means **(a)** applied **(b)** changed **(c)** attached **(d)** carried.

25. He continued to invent. His *ingenious* mind went on and on.
Ingenious (224) means **(a)** fast **(b)** clever **(c)** witty **(d)** tired.

THINKING IT OVER

1. How did Goddard rise above criticism and disappointment? What qualities did he have?

2. The idea of rockets has been around for a thousand years. Why didn't somebody put that idea to practical use earlier?

3. Sometimes a good friend comes along at an important time, as Charles Lindbergh did for Goddard. Did you ever have a friend help you at an important time? Would you care to tell about it?

4. Have you seen pictures of the first moon landing? What do you remember most about these pictures?

5. Scientists say that it is unlikely that UFO's (unidentified flying objects) have come from planets outside our solar system. What do you think? Why is space travel between stars so difficult?

6. Scientists are sending messages into space and listening for messages from space. Scientists say that if intelligent beings live "out there," communication might be possible. Do you agree? Is the effort worthwhile?

7. Have you seen pictures of Jupiter, Saturn, and Saturn's moons as sent back by the *Voyager* spacecrafts? Should we spend the great sums of money needed for information like this? Explain.

8. Some people feel that science is moving too fast for us to control it. The development of nuclear weapons is a constant threat. Pollution increases the dangers of everyday life. On the other hand, some people feel that science has greatly improved our lives. New discoveries in medicine save lives. The computer makes many kinds of work easier. Television has made our leisure time more enjoyable. Robots have made manufacturing more efficient. How do you feel? Is science a blessing or not?

ANOTHER LOOK AT THE QUOTATION

If you want something very badly,
you can achieve it. It may take patience,
very hard work, a real struggle, and a
long time; but it can be done.
                                    MARGO JONES

1. Explain the quotation in your own words.
2. Did Goddard prove in his own life the truth of this quotation? Explain.
3. Have you succeeded in something that took a long time? Tell about it.

WORDS AT YOUR SERVICE—SUFFIXES

Many rockets returned to Earth with a crash and were converted to *useless* junk. (223)

In an earlier chapter you learned the names of word parts: *prefixes, roots, suffixes*. In other chapters you studied some important roots and prefixes. In this chapter we will look at suffixes, those little elements at the end of many common words.

In the sentence quoted above, *useless* has a suffix, *less*, meaning *without*. Though this suffix is tacked onto the end of the word *use*, it is an important part of the word. Something *useless* is *without* the possibility of *use*.

The suffix makes the difference between *useful* and *useless*. Note how the *less* suffix helps give the meaning of the following words.

hopeless—without hope   *childless*—without a child
friendless—without friends   *toothless*—without a tooth
powerless—without power   *homeless*—without a home

Another useful suffix is *able*, meaning *able to be*. Notice what happens when we add this suffix to *use*. Something *usable* is *able to be used*. Now let's add it to two other words. Something *lovable* is *able to be loved*. Something *manageable* is *able to be managed*.

Here are some other helpful suffixes.

Prefix	*Meaning*	*Example*	*Definition of the Word*
er, or	one who	adviser	one who advises
et, ette	small	kitchenette	small kitchen

ful	having the quality of, full of	hopeful	having the quality of hope
hood	state of	motherhood	state of being a mother
ness	state of, condition of	sadness	state of being sad

Fill in the blank in each sentence by supplying the missing suffix from the list above. The number in parentheses tells you how many letters you need. Use your dictionary to help you.

EXAMPLE

Bernie is a tire_____ worker, never showing any sign of needing to rest. (4)
Insert *less*. The complete word is *tireless*.

1. A *small* dining area is called a din_____. (4)
2. *One who* can play the trumpet is called a trumpet_____. (2)
3. The *condition of* being a child is called child_____. (4)
4. When we are joy_____, we are *full of* happiness. (3)
5. Cranki_____ is the *state of* being bad-tempered. (4)

COMPLETING AN OUTLINE

The article on Robert H. Goddard might be outlined in the following way. Five outline items have been omitted. Test your understanding of the structure of the article by following the directions after the outline.

I. The rocket idea
    A. Moon-mad Goddard
    B. History of rockets
    C.

II. Goddard's early years
    A.
    B. Goddard's study of rocket fuels
    C. Difficulties of rocket experimentation

III. Goddard's mature experiments
    A. Encouragement from Charles Lindbergh
    B. Guggenheim grant
    C.
    D. Forerunner of later space ideas

IV. Rockets for war
    A.
    B. The German praise for Goddard's work
    C. Goddard's contribution to the war effort

V. Exploration of space
    A. Landings on Venus and Mars
    B.
    C. Departure into deep space

Fill in the items omitted from the outline. Correctly match the items in column A with the outline numbers in column B, which show where each item belongs in the outline.

A	B

1. The German V-2 rockets
2. Interest in rockets since childhood
3. Ingenuity of Goddard and staff
4. Pictures of Saturn and Jupiter
5. Mistaken ideas about rockets

a. I. C.
b. II. A.
c. III. C.
d. IV. A.
e. V. B.

ANOTHER LOOK

HOW MUCH DO YOU REMEMBER?

1. The two who are associated with science are (a) Susan L. Taylor and Lewis Thomas (b) Twyla Tharp and Robert Goddard (c) Susan L. Taylor and Twyla Tharp (d) Lewis Thomas and Robert Goddard.
2. The person who worked with rockets before World War I was (a) Lewis Thomas (b) Wernher von Braun (c) Robert Goddard (d) Charles Lindbergh.
3. The magazine *Essence* is associated with (a) Twyla Tharp (b) Susan L. Taylor (c) George Balanchine (d) Martha Graham.
4. A National Aeronautics and Space Administration's research area was named after (a) Robert Goddard (b) Lewis Thomas (c) Hermann Oberth (d) Charles Lindbergh.
5. The person who has experimented with new ideas for the dance is (a) Marcia Ann Gillespie (b) Twyla Tharp (c) Lewis Thomas (d) Ntozake Shange.
6. The quality most closely associated with Lewis Thomas is (a) a sense of wonder (b) a quickness

to anger   (c) an interest in being an astronaut
(d) unfriendliness to new ideas.
7. The person who was made fun of, and later apologized to, is   (a) Lewis Thomas   (b) Twyla Tharp
(c) Robert Goddard   (d) Susan Taylor.
8. Which of the following is correctly matched?
(a) Lewis Thomas—astronaut
(b) Twyla Tharp—scientist
(c) Robert Goddard—experimenter
(d) Susan L. Taylor—dancer
9. *The Lives of a Cell* is associated with   (a) Susan L. Taylor   (b) Robert Goddard   (c) Twyla Tharp
(d) Lewis Thomas.
10. The true scientist   (a) is ready to accept new ideas, even if they go against his or her beliefs   (b) tries to publish at least six magazine articles every year
(c) waits for government money before beginning any experiments   (d) attacks other scientists if they disagree.

WHAT IS YOUR OPINION?

1. How did each of the persons in this unit show a willingness to accept new ideas?
2. As you think back, what do you recall the best about each person?
3. Would Lewis Thomas most likely have been interested in Goddard's experiments? Explain.
4. What contribution did Susan L. Taylor and Twyla Tharp make to women's rights?
5. If you were to model yourself after one person in the unit, which would you choose? Why?

THE QUOTATION AND THE UNIT

> *Admitting error clears the score*
> *And proves you wiser than before*
> ARTHUR GUITERMAN

1. Explain the quotation in your own words.
2. Why are people so unwilling to admit their own errors?
3. Did Robert Goddard admit error in his experiments? If so, how did admitting error help him?
4. Can you think of any mistaken ideas of the past that were once accepted as true? Tell about one of them.

UNIT 5

HOLDING TO THE COURSE

Success is a journey, not a destination.
BEN SWEETLAND

A journey requires travelers to hold to their course. In the same way, success usually depends on charting a course and holding to it. The four subjects in this unit have been successful. All four held to their course.

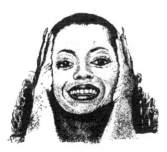

Mary Lou Retton gave up many of the joys of childhood to become a star at the 1984 Olympics. Through disappointments and failures, she held to the course and became a champion.

Tom Selleck spent many years as an unknown actor before he became a successful television star. Eddie Cantor once said, "It takes 20 years to make an overnight success." Tom didn't take 20 years, but he spent a long time on the journey.

Beverly Sills had many reasons to be discouraged, too. At one time she was more famous in Europe than in her native United States. She, too, held to the course and at last became a national treasure.

Diana Ross set her eyes on a goal and pursued that goal. She realized that success does not continue automatically. For more than 20 years she kept her talents before the public.

All four subjects held to the course and proved that courage and patience would win the day.

MARY LOU RETTON:
American Gymnast

*Life is like a ten-speed bike. Most of us
have gears we never use.*
                                    CHARLES SCHULZ

A lifetime of preparation came down to a few seconds. All the hopes and dreams could be won or lost in one moment. It was the 1984 Olympic Games. Mary Lou Retton, 16-year-old American gymnast, hesitated briefly. Then she began to run down the 75-foot track. She picked up speed as she approached the horse. She had planned a layout double-back *somersault* with a double twist. This trick is thought to be too difficult for women. Even most men won't try it. Up she went, twisted, and came down. When she landed, she made history.

Let's look for a moment at some facts leading up to this event. Then we will return to Mary Lou's famous somersault. Until 1984 no American woman had ever won an individual Olympic gymnastics medal of any kind. In 1948 an American women's team had won a bronze medal. In all the years of Olympic gymnastics, that was the best the United States could do. Then came 1984.

Before the Games, the *standout* women's gymnast was Ecaterina Szabo of Rumania. Ecaterina was Rumania's national champion. She had won the European junior championships of 1980 and 1982. She had finished third behind two Soviet gymnasts at the 1983 world meet in Budapest, Hungary. She had collected five 10s, or perfect scores! Since the Soviet teams were not *participating* in the 1984 Olympics, Ecaterina seemed to have the edge.

The gymnastic events are strenuous. There are individual events. In these events, gymnasts can win in their specialties: the floor exercise, the balance beam, the vault, and the uneven parallel bars. Gold, silver, and bronze medals are awarded in each of these. The all-around event combines the others. It eliminates gymnasts who are strong in one or two events and weak in others. The all-around event is the hardest and the most important.

The difference between the individual and the all-around events is shown by the results. In the individuals, Ma

Yanhonig of China and Julianne McNamara of the United States tied for gold medals on the uneven parallel bars. Neither won a medal in the all-around event. Julianne McNamara also won a silver in the floor exercise. Kathy Johnson of the United States won a bronze medal on the balance beam. She did not win a medal in the all-around, though. Lavinia Agache of Rumania won a bronze on the vault, but she did not win a medal in the all-around.

So you see the all-around competition calls for excellent skill in all the events. No one competitor can realistically hope to be tops in *all* events. But the winner has to be a cool competitor.

During the gymnastic competition, a lot of events are going on at the same time. While one athlete is trying to concentrate on the vault, music is playing for someone else's floor exercise. In the middle of one event, the spectators may applaud a fine performance elsewhere. The ability to blot out all distractions is essential.

Going into the all-around event, Mary Lou was given little chance of winning the gold. Experts gave her some chance of winning the silver. Two other powerful Rumanians, Laura Cutina and Simona Pauca, also had excellent chances.

The all-around event is based on individual performances. The gymnasts go into the event with a point total from previous performances. The point scores of four events are added to this total. The gymnasts tackle these events, each in a different order.

Going into the all-around event, Mary Lou had a slight lead. She had a score of 39.525. Ecaterina Szabo had 39.375. On the first round, Ecaterina performed on the balance beam and Mary Lou on the uneven parallel bars.

When Ecaterina came up to the balance beam, she performed incredibly well. She did four back handsprings in a row. No other woman gymnast had ever attempted this *maneuver.* She did a double-back somersault *dismount.* The judges awarded her a perfect score, a 10. At the same moment Mary Lou was performing on the uneven parallel bars. She was awarded a 9.85. At this point the two were tied at 49.375 each.

Mary Lou knew who her toughest competitor would be. Before the all-around event, someone asked her about Ecaterina. "Well, at least she's about my size. You know, we're both about four feet nine inches. I've seen her work, and she's terrific." Mary Lou paused and grinned. "But what she doesn't know about me is that I'm tougher than she is."

Mary Lou would prove that statement soon.

When Mary Lou headed for the beam, Ecaterina began her floor exercise. Ecaterina performed to *The Battle Hymn of the Republic*, a *stirring* piece. At the same time Mary Lou had to work on the balance beam. Ecaterina got a 9.95 from the judges. Mary Lou tried several daring moves, but she scored only a 9.80.

The tide had turned in Ecaterina's favor. The score was 59.325 to 59.175, and there were only two events left.

Was Mary Lou crushed by the turn of events? Not at all. She wasn't keeping score. She knew that Ecaterina was ahead, but as she said later, "I knew she had me edged on points. But I also knew that I had the floor exercise and the vault coming up. And they are my strong events."

The competition had narrowed down to the two girls. Simona Pauca was a distant third, and no one else was really in it.

Mary Lou's floor routine was spectacular. She performed a high double-back somersault, a stunt beyond other women gymnasts. Judges and spectators had to tilt back and look upward at her. *Sports Illustrated* magazine said, "The effect was like a knife thrown at some faraway target." Her ending was equally spectacular, and the judges awarded her a 10.

Not far away, Ecaterina performed well on the vault and earned a 9.90. The difference between their scores had shrunk from 0.15 to 0.05! Only one event remained.

Ecaterina began on the uneven bars. Mary Lou took a quick sideways look and realized that her opponent was doing well. To win the all-around, Mary Lou could get no less than 10 on this event. She would have to be perfect. More than perfect. She would have to display something special, something unusual. In a competition where all the athletes have world-class skill, the winner has to be best among the best. She started down the track.

At the beginning of this selection, we saw Mary Lou perform the vault that made history. All the twists and somersaults can turn to nothing if the dismount is weak. If the gymnast bounces and loses footing on landing, a 10 is impossible. Mary Lou landed firmly, perfectly. She raised her arms and jumped up and down. She knew she had made a perfect score.

She looked at the scoreboard. Ecaterina's excellent performance on the uneven bars had earned her a 9.90, almost perfect. Then came the roar from the spectators. Mary Lou had earned a 10! She had won the all-around event by 0.05 points, a hair's breadth.

Then Mary Lou showed herself a true champion. On the vault the contestants are allowed two jumps. They may then choose the better score of the two. Mary Lou had already made a perfect score. There was no need for her to jump again. But again she stood at the runway and began her swift approach to the horse. As she spun, twisted, and somersaulted, the spectators were awed. She landed perfectly. The judges posted the score—another 10. Perhaps this 10 was meaningless in the competition. But it proved that Mary Lou's success was not a matter of luck.

There were team competitions ahead. The Rumanian team won the team competition. The American team took the silver medal. The Chinese took the bronze. But American women gymnasts had shown the world they could meet the best foreign competitors and win. The American men's gymnastic team also did very well. The team won the gold medals, the first ever for the United States.

Success often comes at a price. It takes sacrifice to become a world-class athlete. From childhood Mary Lou pointed her life toward success in the Olympics. She left her family and boarded away to receive the needed special training. She denied herself many of the pleasures of childhood to train. Even after her Olympic success, she was able to visit her family only once a month.

After the Olympics Mary Lou became the darling of many Americans. She was invited to more events than she could attend. She signed long-term contracts with McDonald's and other corporations. In four months she visited 28 cities. People recognized her everywhere. They asked for her autograph on luggage tags, scraps of paper, even a popsicle stick. She thought she would be unknown in Japan. She said, "I thought I could walk the streets unrecognized, but people would turn around and whisper, 'Retton-san, Retton-san.'"

By the end of 1984, Mary Lou had been on an exhausting merry-go-round, but her heart was still in gymnastics. She planned to continue training with her coach, Bela Karolyi. She hoped to participate in other events, perhaps even the Seoul Olympics in 1988. But whatever her future, no one could take away that golden moment when she scored a perfect 10 to win the 1984 all-around competition in gymnastics.

UNDERSTANDING WHAT YOU HAVE READ

Finding Another Title

1. Another good title for this selection might be (a) The Olympic Games (b) The Thrill of Competition (c) An American Gymnast Makes Olympic History (d) How to Prepare for Olympic Competition.

Getting the Main Idea

2. To win the all-around competition, Mary Lou Retton (a) needed to be incredibly lucky (b) showed her courage by coming from behind (c) outperformed her competitor in all the events (d) had to overcome a secret fear that she would lose.

Finding Details

3. American women gymnasts first won a medal at the Olympics in (a) 1948 (b) 1960 (c) 1980 (d) 1984.
4. All the following are mentioned as part of the women's gymnastic competition EXCEPT (a) balance beam (b) vault (c) floor exercise (d) rings.
5. The gymnast who is mentioned as winning medals for two individual events is (a) Ma Yanhonig (b) Julianne McNamara (c) Laura Cutina (d) Lavinia Agache.
6. The American gymnast who won a bronze medal is (a) Julianne McNamara (b) Kathy Johnson (c) Lavinia Agache (d) not mentioned by name.

7. During the all-around event, Mary Lou was awarded a score of 9.85 on the **(a)** floor exercise **(b)** vault **(c)** uneven parallel bars **(d)** balance beam.
8. Mary Lou Retton and Ecaterina Szabo are alike in their **(a)** coach **(b)** eye color **(c)** height **(d)** scores on the vault.
9. With only one event remaining in the all-around competition, Mary Lou was behind by **(a)** 0.05 **(b)** 0.10 **(c)** 0.15 **(d)** a full point.
10. Bela Karolyi is the name of **(a)** the coach of the Rumanian team **(b)** a judge at the Olympic competition **(c)** the author of a book on gymnastics **(d)** Mary Lou's coach.

Making Inferences

11. A serious obstacle to a perfect performance is **(a)** noise **(b)** dust **(c)** slippery track **(d)** lighting.
12. With only two events left in the all-around event, Ecaterina **(a)** suddenly became weak **(b)** seemed to have an unbeatable lead **(c)** watched Mary Lou on the uneven parallel bars **(d)** had a quiet disagreement with her coach.
13. Of the following, Mary Lou is probably strongest on the **(a)** uneven parallel bars **(b)** balance beam **(c)** trapeze **(d)** vault.
14. The reason Mary Lou took two jumps in her final event was that **(a)** she needed two perfect scores to win **(b)** she felt she could score higher **(c)** she was not confident on the first jump **(d)** she wanted to prove her first jump was no accident.
15. To become a world-class competitor, an athlete most needs **(a)** good luck **(b)** a sense of humor **(c)** complete devotion to the sport **(d)** friends.

Predicting What Happens Next

16. After losing to Mary Lou in the all-around, Ecaterina probably **(a)** gave up gymnastics **(b)** resolved to train even harder **(c)** tried to hire an American coach **(d)** blamed her teammates for the loss.

Deciding on the Order of Events

17. The following events are scrambled. Arrange them in proper order, as they happened. Use letters only.
    (a) Mary Lou visits Japan.
    (b) The American women's gymnastic team wins its first Olympic medal.
    (c) Mary Lou makes two perfect scores on the vault.
    (d) Ecaterina scores 9.95 on the floor exercise.

Inferring Attitude

18. The attitude of the writer of this selection is one of **(a)** obvious admiration **(b)** respect with reservations **(c)** sympathy for an overworked athlete **(d)** moderate interest.

Separating Facts from Opinions

For each of the following, tell whether the statement is a fact (*F*) or an opinion (*O*).
19. Mary Lou won the all-around, but on the basis of her other achievements, Ecaterina is a stronger athlete.
20. Mary Lou earned her highest scores at the end of the all-around.

Understanding Words from Context

21. Mary Lou was not among the choices for winner. Before the Games the *standout* women's gymnast was Ecaterina Szabo of Rumania.
   Standout (242) means   (a) bold   (b) daring   (c) fast (d) leading.

22. Since the Soviet teams were not *participating* in the 1984 Olympics, Ecaterina seemed to have the edge.
   Participating (242) means   (a) battling   (b) traveling   (c) taking part   (d) winning.

23. She did four back handsprings in a row. No other woman gymnast had attempted this *maneuver*.
   Maneuver (243–244) means   (a) fall   (b) trick   (c) reply (d) calling.

24. She did a double-back somersault *dismount* from the beam.
   Dismount (244) means   (a) act of getting off   (b) accident   (c) repetition   (d) twist and turn.

25. Ecaterina performed to *The Battle Hymn of the Republic*, a *stirring* piece.
   Stirring (244) means   (a) quiet   (b) patriotic (c) well-known   (d) exciting.

THINKING IT OVER

1. What does the expression *underdog* mean? Was Ecaterina or Mary Lou the underdog in the Olympics? Is it sometimes an advantage to be the underdog? Explain.

2. Do you recall watching any of the Olympic events on television? Tell what you remember.

3. Men's gymnastic events are quite different from women's. Can you think why this may be so?
4. Were you ever challenged in a way that made you rise above yourself? Tell about it.
5. Is winning sometimes emphasized too much in American sports? Explain how you feel.
6. Suppose you had a chance to become a world-class champion. Suppose, also, that you'd have to devote nearly every waking hour to the sport. Would you take part? Why or why not?

ANOTHER LOOK AT THE QUOTATION

> *Life is like a ten-speed bike. Most of us have gears we never use.*
> CHARLES SCHULZ

1. Explain the quotation in your own words.
2. What are some problems that keep us from doing our best?
3. Does the quotation apply to Mary Lou Retton? Why or why not?

WORDS AT YOUR SERVICE—FOLK ETYMOLOGY

She had planned a layout double-back *somersault* with a double twist. (242)

Everybody knows what a *somersault* is, but little children often call it a "tumble salt." They see the action and think that the athlete is tumbling. Changing an unfamiliar word into something familiar is sometimes called *folk etymology*. Some people call asparagus "sparrow grass." Others call cucumbers "cowcumbers," and *bronchitis* "brownkitis." Indians called a certain animal a *musquash*, but the settlers changed that to *muskrat*. Some children say, "I led the pigeons to the flag" instead of "I pledge allegiance to the flag."

Some of our words have come into existence through folk etymology. People have changed *chaise longue* (long chair) to *chaise lounge*. A *hiccup* has nothing to do with a *cough*, but people thought it did. Now we have the spelling *hiccough*. *Shamefast* became *shamefaced* because people thought the shame would show on the face. A cheese dish, *Welsh rabbit*, has been changed to *Welsh rarebit*.

Often folk etymology helps our language grow.

TOM SELLECK:
Television Star

*Perseverance is not a long race; it is
many short races one after another*
WALTER ELLIOTT

"There was as much excitement outside the auditorium as inside. The two people who aroused the most fan interest were Prince and Tom Selleck."

Roger Ebert and Gene Siskel, film critics, were talking about the 1985 Academy Awards ceremonies in Hollywood. The singer Prince had arrived with motorcycles as escort. He had dressed in a colorful costume that caught every eye. His arrival created a sensation.

Tom Selleck arrived with no *fanfare*. He was dressed in a simple tuxedo. But when the fans saw him, they went wild. There was something about this mild, modest, easygoing man that appealed to everyone.

Tom was not eligible for an Oscar, the statue given as an award. He was there merely to introduce some of the nominees. If the audience had been able to award an Oscar on the spot, Tom Selleck would have had one!

In 1985 *People* magazine listed the best-paid performers in many entertainment fields. Tom Selleck was the highest-paid television actor. Earnings may not always reflect an artist's ability, but they always reflect the artist's popularity. Tom Selleck's popularity was real and well earned.

In 1980–1981 Tom became an international success with the television series *Magnum, P.I.* Tom was in his late thirties by the time he became so prominent as Magnum. He did not suddenly fall into a good part without preparation and experience. He had worked hard and long to reach the peak. He had stayed on course through many disappointments.

Tom Selleck was born in Detroit, Michigan, on January 29, 1945. He was the second of four children. When he was four, his family moved from Detroit to Sherman Oaks, California. The family was close and the parents had a strong influence on the children. Each child received a gold watch at 21 for not smoking, drinking, or swearing. This conservative influence shaped Tom's life-style.

Tom was an outstanding athlete in high school. He won an athletic scholarship to the University of Southern California. A professional athletic career might have been possible for him. The famous Yankee outfielder Mickey Mantle once said that Tom could have been a major league slugger.

Tom's early sports activities were a *forerunner* of his activities today. At 6 feet 4 inches and 200 pounds, Tom stays in excellent physical shape. Even today he enjoys swimming, sailing, and jogging. He plays regularly with a nationally ranked volleyball team in Hawaii. He's not on the team because of his fame. As he says, "No one cares if I'm on TV. I'm off the team if I don't perform. It's nice to get away from business and it's a neat way to get stuff out of your system."

In 1967 something happened that shaped Tom's life. Because of his good looks and excellent physical condition, Tom received a modeling assignment. He appeared in a Pepsi–Cola commercial as a basketball player. He signed an acting contract with Twentieth–Century–Fox that same year, but his progress was slow.

He did other commercials, but he didn't get an acting role for three years. Then his roles in these early movies were small. Critics didn't notice him. In 1972 he had a solid role in a low-budget movie called *Daughters of Satan.* Critics singled out his performance for praise.

He had bit parts in some big-budget movies like *Midway* and *Coma.* But he did not become famous at that time. He tried television and appeared in a soap opera and a television series. But during the 1970s, most of Tom Selleck's income came from commercials.

Tom made over fifty commercials. These provided needed income, though Tom never liked acting in them. Still the commercials made him well known. Tom's rugged good looks also appeared in magazines and on television.

Plans for various television programs fell through. Then CBS considered a new detective series. The popular *Hawaii Five–O* was going off the air. In the new series Magnum would be a private detective in Hawaii. Using Hawaii would allow the producers wonderful settings for the action. Who would play Magnum?

Our lives sometimes depend on little things. Lorne Green tried out for *Bonanza* on the advice of someone he met casually in a barber shop. His role in *Bonanza* made him famous. A chance word or a wrong turn may change a person's life. Tom Selleck's career hung on a chance, too.

CBS executives remembered a part Tom Selleck had played in an episode of *The Rockford Files*. They offered Tom the role of Magnum. Tom had waited a long time for such a break, but he didn't jump at it. He thought about the character. He thought he could make it better. Finally he came up with a suggestion.

As Selleck explained in a *Saturday Evening Post* interview, "They agreed to redo the Magnum character— he would not always get the girl, and he would occasionally blunder badly, and so forth."

The idea worked beautifully. The public fell in love with the character of Magnum. As an article in *Current Biography* reports, "The revised script, which Selleck liked very much, turned Tom Magnum—a former naval intelligence officer and Vietnam war veteran—into an easygoing, *fallible* private eye with a touch of *fatalism* and an engaging sense of humor. The glamor came from Selleck's romantic looks and from the setting, a lavish Hawaiian estate, that belonged to an absent novelist."

The producers surrounded Magnum with a good cast, including John Hillerman and Roger E. Mosley. Despite the seriousness of some of the plots, there was a comic element that kept the scripts lively.

Tom had a good break when he was picked for Magnum.

He had a bad break soon after. As *Magnum, P.I.* was going into production, Tom Selleck was unexpectedly offered the lead role in *Raiders of the Lost Ark*. (See page 42.) This picture went on to become one of the most profitable of all time. If Tom had landed the role of Indiana Jones, who knows where his career might have taken him?

CBS refused to release Selleck from his obligation to play Magnum. An actors' strike delayed the release of *Magnum P.I.* till December 1980, but by then the Indiana Jones role had gone to Harrison Ford.

Television critics are a severe group, but *Magnum, P.I.* got good reviews. By its second season it had become one of the most-watched shows on the air, often among the top ten. Even the usually *biting* critic Tom Carson called Selleck "a master of television behavior in much the same way Clark Gable was a master of movie behavior." Carson also liked the light touch Tom gave to the part.

Tom didn't want to be known only for his role as Magnum. A series takes up most of an actor's energies, but Tom decided to work outside the role, too. Though he worked eighty-hour, six-day weeks for most of the year, he used his April-to-July break to take on other assignments.

During his first seasonal break, in 1981, he starred in a TV movie, *Divorce Wars*. During his second break, in 1982, he played the lead in a feature film, *High Road to China*. The next year he starred in *Lassiter*. He continued to take on other roles, in addition to his role as Magnum. Other actors admired his work, comparing him to Clark Gable and Humphrey Bogart.

Being a celebrity isn't all fun. Tom is a modest, conservative person. He doesn't particularly like the limelight. Reporters, gossip columnists, and too-eager fans can be a bother. He realizes he loses much of his privacy by being famous. But he does try to keep some part of his life private. He is not conceited in any way, not impressed with his own importance.

He is a serious actor and takes the acting profession seriously. Still, he does keep a sense of humor about it. After all, he says, "I don't like to get too *reverent* about it. I don't think we're curing cancer."

UNDERSTANDING WHAT YOU HAVE READ

Finding Another Title

1. Another good title for this selection might be **(a)** Tom Selleck: Success Story **(b)** Television vs. Movies **(c)** A Popular Person **(d)** Hard Work in Commercials.

Getting the Main Idea

2. Tom Selleck **(a)** was an excellent college athlete **(b)** kept the same pleasant personality throughout years of struggle and success **(c)** was offered a major role in *Bonanza* **(d)** was an overnight sensation in his first movie.

Finding Details

3. Tom Selleck's family moved from Detroit to Sherman Oaks, California **(a)** on January 29, 1945 **(b)** when Tom was four years old **(c)** because Tom's father had a movie offer **(d)** before Tom was born.
4. The famous baseball player mentioned in the selection is **(a)** Roger Maris **(b)** Mickey Mantle **(c)** Harrison Ford **(d)** Willie Mays.
5. All the following are mentioned as sports played by Tom Selleck EXCEPT **(a)** swimming **(b)** volleyball **(c)** baseball **(d)** soccer.
6. The character of Magnum in *Magnum, P.I.* is **(a)** a Vietnam war veteran **(b)** a news reporter **(c)** an army colonel **(d)** a Californian.
7. John Hillerman is **(a)** a movie director **(b)** a writer **(c)** an actor **(d)** a producer.
8. Tom Selleck was not able to take the role offered him in **(a)** *The Rockford Files* **(b)** *Daughters of Satan* **(c)** *Midway* **(d)** *Raiders of the Lost Ark.*
9. *Magnum, P.I.* was first released in **(a)** 1967 **(b)** 1972 **(c)** 1980 **(d)** 1981.
10. Each of the following is a critic EXCEPT **(a)** Tom Carson **(b)** Roger Ebert **(c)** Roger E. Mosley **(d)** Gene Siskel.

Making Inferences

11. A gold watch **(a)** reminds Tom of his parents' teachings **(b)** was given to Tom after three successful years of *Magnum, P.I.* **(c)** was part of a famous commercial with Tom Selleck **(d)** was once used by Indiana Jones.

12. Tom changed the character of Magnum to make him more (a) kind (b) perfect (c) quiet (d) interesting.

13. Indiana Jones is a character in (a) *Raiders of the Lost Ark* (b) *Coma* (c) *Magnum, P.I.* (d) *Daughters of Satan.*

14. Tom Selleck does not work for *Magnum, P.I.* in the month of (a) January (b) June (c) October (d) December.

15. A good word to describe Tom Selleck is (a) *reckless* (b) *modest* (c) *extravagant* (d) *lazy.*

Predicting What Happens Next

16. After the fourth year of shooting *Magnum, P.I.*, Tom Selleck probably decided on his break to (a) take it easy (b) go back to making commercials (c) look for an additional acting job (d) retire.

Deciding on the Order of Events

17. The following events are scrambled. Arrange them in proper order, as they happened. Use letters only.
    (a) Tom gets the lead role in *Magnum, P.I.*
    (b) Tom plays a role in *The Rockford Files.*
    (c) Tom appears in a Pepsi–Cola commercial.
    (d) Tom appears in a film, *High Road to China.*

Inferring Tone

18. Tom's comment about acting and curing cancer (258) is intended to be (a) lighthearted (b) serious (c) puzzling (d) irritable.

Separating Facts from Opinions

For each of the following, tell whether the statement is a fact (*F*) or an opinion (*O*).
19. Tom Selleck was offered a part taken by Harrison Ford.
20. Tom Selleck is one of the nicest leading men in Hollywood.

Understanding Words from Context

21. Unlike Prince, who arrived with a motorcycle escort, Tom arrived with no *fanfare*.
    Fanfare (254) means   (a) struggle   (b) news reporter   (c) companion   (d) fuss.
22. Because Tom did not think Magnum should be perfect, the script turned Magnum into "an easygoing, *fallible* private eye."
    Fallible (256) means   (a) easily discouraged   (b) able to make mistakes   (c) having a charming personality   (d) looking for faults in others.
23. Magnum is a relaxed fellow with a touch of *fatalism* that prevents him from taking his actions too seriously.
    Fatalism (256) means   (a) disaster   (b) worry   (c) acceptance of fate   (d) desire for riches.
24. Some feared being reviewed by Tom Carson, since he is usually a *biting* critic.
    Biting (257) means   (a) severe   (b) humorous   (c) unfair   (d) cheerful.
25. Although Tom takes acting seriously, he doesn't like to get too *reverent* about it.
    Reverent (258) means   (a) dramatic   (b) worried   (c) respectful   (d) angry.

THINKING IT OVER

1. How did Tom Selleck, throughout his life, show the same steady purpose?
2. Does luck play a role in life? Has luck ever influenced your life? Tell about it.
3. Have you ever seen *Magnum, P.I.*? Did you enjoy it? Explain.
4. What are some of the disadvantages of being famous? How did Tom handle these?
5. Some films are made for movie theaters and some are made for television. Are the two types of films different? Are they intended for different audiences? Explain.
6. Every actor must be ready to accept criticism and not let it bother him or her. Not everyone will like a certain person or a particular movie. How can an actor benefit from criticism?

ANOTHER LOOK AT THE QUOTATION

> *Perseverance is not a long race; it is*
> *many short races one after another.*
> WALTER ELLIOTT

1. *Perseverance* means sticking to something. Explain in your own words what the quotation means to you.
2. Do you find that most problems tend to be *many and small*, rather than *very few but serious*? Explain.
3. Why do we sometimes fail to stick to something we should be doing? Can sticking to a job be taught? How?

WORDS AT YOUR SERVICE—LITTLE WORDS IN BIG WORDS

Tom's early sports activities were a *forerunner* of his activities today. (255)

Sometimes long words are easier to understand than short ones. A short word like *fray* is harder than a long word like *uncontrollable*. There are no clues to the meaning of *fray* in the word itself. There are many clues to the meaning of *uncontrollable* in the word itself. There, in the middle of the long word, is the easy word *control*. *Uncontrollable* means *not able to be controlled*. *Fray* means *a fight*, as in *go into the fray*. But there are no hints in the word itself.

Like *uncontrollable, forerunner* is not a short word, but it is an easy word. It means *something that goes before*, and the clues are right there before us. Tom's athletic activities in college were signs of things to come—signs of his activities today.

Try your skill at guessing the meaning of longer words. Match a meaning in column B with a word in column A.

A	B
1. cannonade	a. weakness
2. condemnation	b. strict person
3. disciplinarian	c. firing of guns
4. forethought	d. disapproval
5. humidifier	e. strangeness
6. infirmity	f. ability to be sold
7. marketability	g. lack of loyalty
8. miscalculation	h. device for moistening
9. peculiarity	i. planning ahead
10. unfaithfulness	j. jumping to wrong conclusions

COMPLETING AN OUTLINE

The article on Tom Selleck might be outlined in the following way. Five outline items have been omitted. Test your understanding of the structure of the article by following the directions after the outline.

I. Introduction to Tom Selleck
   A.
   B. Financial success

II. Early years
   A.
   B. Conservative upbringing
   C. Ability as athlete
   D. Possibility of career in sports

III. First career moves
   A.
   B. Small roles in movies
   C. Successful career in commercials

IV. Stardom
   A.
   B. Offer of leading role in *Raiders of the Lost Ark*
   C. Television movies
   D. Leading roles in Hollywood films

V. Personality
   A.
   B. Seriousness combined with sense of humor

Fill in the items omitted from the outline. Correctly match the items in column A with the outline numbers in column B, which show where each item belongs in the outline.

A		B	
1.	Selection for role in *Magnum*	a.	I.A.
2.	Modesty	b.	II.A.
3.	Birth in Detroit in 1945	c.	III.A.
4.	Popularity at Oscar ceremonies	d.	IV.A.
5.	Modeling for Pepsi–Cola ad	e.	V.A.

BEVERLY SILLS:
Famous Singer

*People seldom see the halting and pain-
ful steps by which the most insignificant
success is achieved.*
ANNE SULLIVAN MACY

When you go to the movies, do you picture yourself in the film? Do you say to yourself, "I want to be like the star in the movie"?

Most young people have dreams about the future. In the early 1930s, Beverly Sills had a dream, too. Though she was not yet in school, she had a talent for singing. Once Beverly and her mother attended a concert by the famous opera singer Lily Pons. The young Beverly wanted to sit up very close. She said, "I want to see what she does with her mouth. Mamma, someday I want to sing like Lily Pons."

Beverly achieved her ambition. The years that followed her seeing Lily Pons brought her to the top of her profession. Like Lily Pons, she sang at the Metropolitan Opera. She won praise and fame around the world. The name *Beverly Sills* became as well known in the Milan Opera House as in her native country. How did she achieve all this success?

In many movies about performers, fame comes overnight. A stroke of luck brings a shy country boy to the notice of a song writer. The boy records the song. He becomes an instant sensation. A starstruck girl from the Midwest comes to Hollywood to make her fortune. She is noticed by a famous producer and becomes a star. Is this how Beverly Sills achieved success?

Writers and artists rely on real-life situations for ideas. People say that art imitates life. Sometimes, however, the opposite is true. Unusual and unexpected things do happen. How many times have you said to yourself, "If I hadn't seen it with my own eyes, I wouldn't believe it?"

Often, though, success depends not so much on luck as on hard work. It comes after *setbacks* and hardships. This is what is meant by the saying, "He paid his dues." Beverly Sills worked hard to reach the top. She "paid her dues."

Beverly Sills was born Belle Miriam Silverman on May 25, 1929, in Brooklyn, New York. She was the youngest of three children. Her two brothers later became successful in their chosen fields. But no one could foresee how famous Beverly would become.

Beverly's friends and associates are still warmed by her personality. That warmth was apparent even in the little child. Her mother once said, "She's been bubbly all her life—as eager, as willing, as loving now as ever." Even today her friends call her Bubbles.

Beverly was only three years old when she first won praise for her singing. She won first prize in the "Miss Beautiful Baby Contest of 1932" at a Brooklyn park. During this contest, she showed incredible talent singing a catchy song, "The Wedding of Jack and Jill."

Beverly's mother realized that her daughter was special. She provided voice and dance lessons. These lessons were not wasted. Before she was ten, Beverly performed professionally on radio. In 1938 she was in a film.

Beverly's private life was colored by her interest in music. Before the age of seven she had memorized 22 operatic *arias*. These solo selections are often the highlights of the operas. They are difficult to perform well. Her mother had an eleven-disc recording of the famous singer Galli-Curci. Beverly imitated the singing. She even imitated the Italian, in which the arias were sung.

Beverly was not a spoiled child who lived a one-track life. Not at all. She went to public school and was liked by her friends. When she graduated from Public School 91 in 1942, she was honored by her classmates. They voted her the "prettiest," the "most likely to succeed," and the "one with the most personality." These students saw the future.

Throughout this period, Beverly was busy. She took daily French and Italian lessons, for many operas are sung in these languages. She worked with a voice coach every day. She took weekly piano lessons, too! By the time she was 15, she had mastered 20 operatic roles.

Beverly became a full-time professional in 1945. She toured with a national light-opera group and experienced all the difficulties of touring. There were long trips and exhausting travel. The difficulties had some good results, though. She was learning throughout this period. She played half a dozen principal roles in Gilbert and Sullivan operettas. Then came leads in operettas like *Rosemarie* and *The Merry Widow*.

In 1947 Beverly undertook her first role in grand opera. She played the gypsy Frasquita in Bizet's *Carmen* with the Philadelphia Civic Opera. She was excellent in the role, but national recognition and fame were still many years away.

The years ahead were a time of disappointment and struggle. Her father's death in 1949 brought financial hardship to the struggling young singer. She sang in a private club to make ends meet. She toured with an opera company from coast to coast, but money was never plentiful.

She became an able performer in *La Traviata* and *Carmen*. At the San Francisco Opera in 1953 she was highly praised for her performance as Helen of Troy in another opera. These successes did not open doors for her, though.

For three years she *auditioned* unsuccessfully for the New York City Opera. At last, in 1955, she was accepted into the company. On October 29, 1955, she was a magnificent Rosalinde in Johann Strauss's *Die Fledermaus*. Music critic Francis D. Perkins called her "an accomplished singing actress." But the road ahead was still rocky.

On April 3, 1958, she won universal critical praise in New York for a role in *The Ballad of Baby Doe*. Did this success guarantee her a role on the stage of the great Metropolitan Opera? Unfortunately, no. That success had to wait 17 more years.

Beverly Sills married Peter Buckeley Greenough in 1956. Both children of that marriage were found to have disabilities. In 1961 Beverly Sills gave up her career to devote time to the children. This was a period of bitterness and grief, but Beverly's natural optimism brought her through the ordeal. Her later leadership on behalf of disabled children arose from her personal experiences.

After a while her husband and friends urged her to return to the concert stage. Gradually she took on more singing challenges. She sang with the Boston Opera Company, with the New Orleans Opera, and again with the New York City Opera. When she played in New York, Winthrop Sargeant, music critic for the *New Yorker* magazine, called her the "prima donna," the principal singer of the company.

With the New York City Opera she played role after role. In commenting on her performance as Manon in 1969, Sargeant wrote, "If I were recommending the wonders of New York to a tourist, I would place Beverly Sills at the top of the list—way ahead of such things as the Statue of Liberty and the Empire State Building."

A French writer once commented, "No man is a hero to his valet," or personal attendant. In other words, we sometimes fail to appreciate the people who are closest to us. In the late 1960s Beverly became famous in Europe. She was enthusiastically received in Milan, London, and Berlin. But she was still not invited to sing at the Metropolitan Opera.

At last came the long-awaited moment. On April 8, 1975, Beverly made her Metropolitan Opera debut as Pamira in *The Siege of Corinth*. The cheers were overwhelming. She received an 18-minute *ovation*. The critics praised her performance. Andrew Porter, another critic for the *New Yorker,* called it a performance of "uncommon merit." New York critics are not easy to please, but Beverly had won the day.

Success followed success, in New York and across the country. Beverly had truly reached the heights and had sung "like Lily Pons." But what does one do after reaching the top? Beverly reached for a still higher peak. In 1979 she became director of the New York City Opera.

The decision to take on the *demanding* job of director forced her to end her active singing career. She looked to a new challenge. The New York City Opera had been in financial difficulties, and the future looked hopeless. This challenge didn't stop Beverly.

Beverly saw different roles for the 100-year-old Metropolitan Opera and much younger New York City Opera. The New York City Opera could be more daring. It could use less-known local singers and escape the high salaries of internationally famous opera stars. It could try experiments, like projecting English subtitles above the stage. This device enabled opera-goers to follow the story more closely.

Beverly made other changes. She moved the dates of the opera season to avoid too much conflict with the Metropolitan Opera season. She tried new operas and new ways of staging old operas. She avoided the grand and expensive sets, or scenery, of the Metropolitan. She lowered ticket prices to attract a larger audience.

After years of struggle, Beverly could look back on a financially stronger New York City Opera. She had come a long way from that Lily Pons concert 50 years before, but she always aimed higher.

Beverly doesn't restrict herself to music alone. She is active in many good causes. She served as chairwoman of the Mothers' March on Birth Defects and as an adviser to the National Endowment for the Arts. Though she takes on many jobs, she remains enthusiastic, warm, and open. She has proved herself to be a national treasure.

UNDERSTANDING WHAT YOU HAVE READ

Finding Another Title

1. Another good title for this selection might be (a) The Importance of Music Lessons (b) Opera in America (c) A Life Devoted to Music (d) The Importance of Luck.

Getting the Main Idea

2. Throughout her successful life, Beverly Sills combined the qualities of (a) courage and enthusiasm (b) nervousness and carelessness (c) intelligence and indecision (d) shyness and talent.

Finding Details

3. Lily Pons (a) was a friend of Beverly Sills's family (b) encouraged Beverly to audition for the New York City Opera (c) ran the Boston Opera (d) inspired Beverly in her career.
4. "The Wedding of Jack and Jill" (a) brought Beverly her first prize (b) is a song Beverly wrote while in elementary school (c) is a song from an opera (d) came from a famous film.
5. Beverly Sills sang the role of Helen of Troy in (a) Milan (b) New York (c) San Francisco (d) New Orleans.

6. It took three years of auditions for Beverly to win a role (a) in Bizet's *Carmen* (b) at the New York City Opera (c) at the San Francisco Opera (d) in *The Merry Widow.*

7. Peter Buckeley Greenough is (a) a former director of the San Francisco Opera (b) a music critic (c) a music conductor (d) Beverly's husband.

8. In mid-career Beverly retired from the stage (a) to rest her voice (b) because of a serious illness (c) to take care of her children (d) at her husband's request.

9. Beverly Sills received an eighteen-minute ovation for (a) the role of Manon (b) a performance in London (c) her debut at the Metropolitan Opera (d) *The Ballad of Baby Doe.*

10. Beverly became director of the New York City Opera in (a) 1961 (b) 1969 (c) 1975 (d) 1979.

Making Inferences

11. The expression "she paid her dues" (267) suggests that Beverly (a) joined the musicians' union (b) worked hard to reach success (c) knew how to use other people for her benefit (d) was always good to her fellow workers.

12. As a child, Beverly imitated the singing of the famous Galli-Curci to (a) amuse her mother (b) pass the time (c) take the singer's place (d) try her own skill as a singer.

13. For opera singers probably the peak of success is singing (a) on a weekly television series (b) in a good movie (c) at the New York City Opera (d) at the Metropolitan Opera.

14. When the Metropolitan Opera finally brought Beverly on the great stage, her friends might have said, **(a)** "It's about time." **(b)** "I'm worried that Beverly might not make it." **(c)** "She would be better off with the New York City Opera." **(d)** "This will ruin her chances to make a film."

15. The reason for one of the changes Beverly made at the New York City Opera is that she believed **(a)** many people preferred local singers to international stars **(b)** many opera lovers could not afford the higher-priced tickets **(c)** New York City should have its own company **(d)** people were tired of the old operas.

Predicting What Happens Next

16. After Beverly returned to the stage, her husband most likely **(a)** kept encouraging her **(b)** tried to get her to stop **(c)** refused to take the children to see her **(d)** regretted her choice.

Deciding on the Order of Events

17. The following events are scrambled. Arrange them in proper order, as they happened. Use letters only.
    (a) Beverly sings the role of Rosalinde.
    (b) Beverly is married.
    (c) Beverly is voted the "most likely to succeed."
    (d) Beverly sings with the Philadelphia Civic Opera.

Inferring Attitude

18. The attitude of Winthrop Sargeant toward Beverly Sills's singing (270) is one of **(a)** admiration **(b)** scorn **(c)** insincere flattery **(d)** uncertainty.

Separating Facts from Opinions

For each of the following, tell whether the statement is a fact (*F*) or an opinion (*O*).

19. Beverly Sills is the greatest American singing star of the past 20 years.
20. Beverly Sills served as chairwoman of the Mothers' March on Birth Defects.

Understanding Words from Context

21. Final success comes after *setbacks* and hardships.
    Setbacks (267) means **(a)** challenges **(b)** battles **(c)** victories **(d)** defeats.
22. Before the age of seven she had memorized 22 operatic *arias*. These solo selections are often the highlights of the operas.
    Arias (268) means **(a)** dances **(b)** skits **(c)** airs for a single voice **(d)** dramas.
23. She kept trying for a part. For three years she *auditioned* unsuccessfully for the New York City Opera.
    Auditioned (269) means **(a)** performed **(b)** sang **(c)** tried out **(d)** appealed.
24. The cheers were overwhelming; she received an 18-minute *ovation*.
    Ovation (270) means **(a)** long speech **(b)** burst of applause **(c)** musical number **(d)** fireworks display.
25. The decision to take on the *demanding* job forced her to end her active singing career.
    Demanding (271) means **(a)** hard **(b)** irritating **(c)** interesting **(d)** cruel.

THINKING IT OVER

1. A life without challenges and occasional defeats is likely to be dull. How did the difficulties in her life help Beverly achieve her goals? Explain.
2. Have you had unexpected setbacks in your own life? How did you handle them? As you look back, would you have done anything differently? Explain.
3. Do you think that sometimes "Life imitates art"? Explain. Does the selection imply that life imitated art in Beverly's life? Explain.
4. How did Beverly's somewhat normal childhood help her in her adult life?
5. A common proverb claims that familiarity breeds contempt, or lack of respect. What does this proverb mean? Do you agree with it? Why or why not?

ANOTHER LOOK AT THE QUOTATION

> *People seldom see the halting and painful steps by which the most insignificant success is achieved.*
>
> ANNE SULLIVAN MACY

1. Explain the quotation in your own words.
2. How does the quotation apply to the life of Beverly Sills?
3. The word *insignificant* means *unimportant* or *barely noticeable*. How can success be insignificant?
4. Do you know the story of Helen Keller? She was the remarkable woman who learned to lead a full and productive life even though she was blind and deaf. Anne Sullivan Macy was her teacher. Why was Macy especially qualified to say what she did?

WORDS AT YOUR SERVICE—METAPHORS

These successes did not open doors for her, though. (269)

Is the author talking about real doors here? You certainly don't picture someone refusing to open actual doors for Beverly Sills. This is an example of *figurative language*. You use figurative language often, though you don't realize you are doing so.

As you read the following examples, try to visualize the expressions. Look at the expressions afresh and see the picture in each.

fly off the handle	a tower of strength
hit the roof	drop her eyes to the floor
eye of a hurricane	throw him a warning glance
die laughing	run out of steam
arm of the sea	iron will

A *metaphor* is a type of figurative language. It is an indirect comparison between basically unlike things. For example, read the following sentence:

The fullback was a *giant* standing in the way of the other team.

When you read these words, you don't think that the fullback was actually a giant. But you know that he appeared this way to the opposing team. You see the picture, or hidden comparison, in the words. But you also understand the literal, or actual, meaning of the words. You know that in the example above, the word *giant* means that the fullback was very big.

For each of the sentences on page 278, choose the words that best express the literal, or actual, meaning of the metaphor.

1. Beverly was not a spoiled child who lived a *one-track* life.
   One-track means (a) single direction (b) quick-paced (c) unhappy (d) normal.
2. Winthrop Sargeant said Beverly was one of "the *wonders* of New York . . . way ahead of such things as the Statue of Liberty and the Empire State Building."
   Wonders means (a) buildings (b) tourist sights (c) pleasures (d) statues.
3. Beverly was not content with success; she reached for a *still higher peak*.
   Still higher peak means (a) additional achievement (b) failure (c) review (d) happiness.
4. The road to success was not a series of *open doors* for Beverly to walk through.
   Open doors means (a) easy successes (b) exits (c) entrances (d) roadblocks.
5. The road ahead of Beverly was still *rocky*.
   Rocky means (a) pebbly (b) easy (c) difficult (d) harsh.

COMPLETING AN OUTLINE

The article on Beverly Sills might be outlined in the following way. Five items have been omitted. Test your understanding of the structure of the article by following the directions after the outline.

I. The early years (1929–1945)
   A.
   B. Warm personality
   C. Early recognition
   D. Many lessons

II. The young professional (1945–1955)
   A. Struggles on the road
   B.
   C. Unsuccessful auditions for the New York City Opera

III. Success at last (1955–1975)
   A. Debut in *Die Fledermaus*
   B. Marriage
   C.
   D. Return to stage
   E.

IV. Career at the peak (1975 on)
   A. Debut in the Metropolitan Opera
   B.
   C. Acceptance of new challenges

Fill in the items omitted from the outline. Correctly match the items in column A with the outline numbers in column B, which show where each item belongs in the outline.

A	B
1. Debut in grand opera	a. I. A.
2. Director of the New York City Opera	b. II. B.
	c. III. C.
3. Young dreams	d. III. E.
4. Devotion to children	e. IV. B.
5. Recognition abroad	

DIANA ROSS:
Star of Pop Music

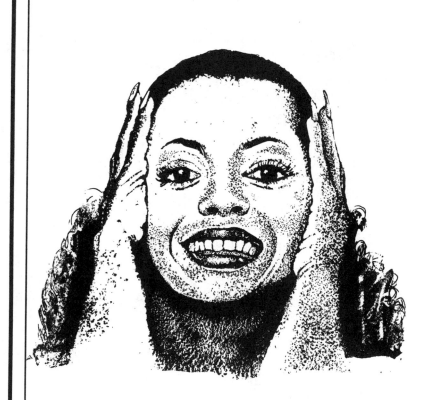

When I'm pushing myself, testing myself, that's when I'm happiest. That's when the rewards are greatest.

SISSY SPACEK

In 1985 the most famous stars of popular music gathered in Los Angeles to cut a disc. They were giving their services free to help the starving children of Africa. That record, *We Are the World,* became one of the most successful albums of its time. One of the leading stars at this event was Diana Ross.

Popular music is a rapidly changing field. Many new performers catch the public's eye. They are in demand. Their music quickly rises to the top of the charts. They enjoy a brief period of popularity. Then they sink out of sight just as quickly. Their music is replaced by the songs of another singer or group. It is a world of fierce competition. A singer's days of fame and fortune may be brief.

Diana Ross is one of the shining exceptions. She became one of the most successful singers of all time. Her career has lasted for many years, not just months. She was a hit in the 1960s. Twenty years later she was still first in her fans' hearts. In the 1980s a concert in New York City's Central Park drew 350,000 enthusiastic fans.

Sometimes a person's success depends almost entirely on luck. Not Diana. She worked hard for her success. Her life story is the American dream come true. She did not live an easy life. She did not come from a family of entertainers. She created her own image.

The name *Diana* was a mistake on her birth certificate. Her parents named her *Diane.* Her family and friends call her *Diane,* but *Diana* is the name she uses in her work.

Diana was born in Detroit, Michigan, on March 26, 1944. She was the second oldest of six children. She had two sisters and three brothers. While she was growing up, the family lived in a low-income housing project in a poor section of Detroit. But Diana never felt unhappy. She later said, "I suppose life was difficult, but as a child I didn't notice those things. . . . I never thought of it being a *ghetto* when I was there."

She had her first taste of singing in public in a church choir. Her grandfather was a minister, and all his children were brought up to sing in church. Diana followed the tradition. She had very little voice training. The choir director of the church provided a little help, and a cousin coached her in pop singing. Otherwise her talents were natural and not professionally created.

Diana was a standout at Cass Technical High School. She studied dress design, costume illustration, and the use of cosmetics. She was an excellent dress designer. Her classmates voted her the best-dressed girl in the class. Diana made most of her own clothes. In addition, she was an excellent athlete, a successful member of the swimming team.

Did Diana do any singing outside the church choir? She had two close friends who were also interested in singing: Mary Wilson and Florence Ballard. The three often *harmonized* on street corners and sang at parties. They called themselves the *Primettes*. They were good enough to make about $15 a week. This is a small amount even by today's standards. It is a very tiny amount when compared with Diana's later earnings. But it showed Diana that people would pay to hear her sing.

It was at this time that Diana had her first setback. She tried out for a part in a high school musical. She was turned down. The teacher in charge told her, "You have a nice voice, but it's nothing special." Someone less courageous than Diana might have given up. But Diana believed in her heart that the teacher was wrong. She stuck to the course and tried harder than ever.

At about the same time, an important opportunity arose. In 1959, Berry Gordy, Jr., took a step that changed modern popular music. He was a former worker on a Detroit automobile assembly line. He thought that black singers did not have the opportunities they deserved. Detroit is

often called the "motor town." Gordy took the two words
and created the Motown Record Corporation.

Motown opened up doors for black singers. Geoffrey
Cannon, critic of the *Guardian,* wrote a history of pop
music. He paid tribute to Motown in this way: "Black
harmony music was first sung in church; but most of the
black groups who were successful up to the 1960's in
America were owned by white businessmen who turned
their singing towards comedy or novelty." He then went
on to congratulate Berry Gordy, a black businessman, for
showing how Gospel music can be attractive to a national
audience.

Diana knew about Motown and kept after Gordy. While
she was still in high school, she asked Gordy to hire the
Primettes. She took a job as a secretarial assistant at
Motown for two weeks. She spoke to Gordy often.

Gordy began to listen to his assistant. He used the
Primettes as background singers in recordings. They provided background for singers like Marvin Gaye, Mary
Wells, and the Shirelles. Then he decided to feature the
three girls on their own.

Gordy didn't like the name the *Primettes. Prime* means
first, but the sound of *Primettes* didn't appeal to him. *Supreme* also means *first, best.* He renamed Diana's group
the *Supremes.* This name made music history.

Gordy didn't believe that a star is made overnight. His
record company had a department for training his singers.
They were taught how to walk, how to move, how to dress,
how to behave. This training gave the Supremes the poise
they needed for national fame.

Critic Geoffrey Cannon admired Gordy. He said, "Gordy
poured all his energy and money into what has been his
most dramatic social achievement: getting *universal* acceptance, by means of Diana Ross, of the idea that black
is beautiful."

The Supremes soon cut their first record. It was a single "I Want a Guy." It created little stir. They cut eight more. Again there was little notice of the new singers.

Then Gordy gave them new writers. Eddie Holland, Lamont Dozier, and Brian Holland knew how to showcase the special talents of the Supremes. In 1964 the Supremes had their first hit, "Where Did Our Love Go?" Diana sang the lead. Florence and Mary sang the background.

The Supremes were on their way. "Where Did Our Love Go?" was the third Motown single to reach the number-one spot. The record sold 2 million copies. More important still, it made the Supremes nationally known.

In the next year the Supremes had five more top-spot singles. The titles were "Baby Love," "Come See About Me," "Stop in the Name of Love," "Back in My Arms Again," and "I Hear a Symphony." They were the only singing group in history to earn six *consecutive* Gold Records. A Gold Record is one that sells a million or more copies. By 1965 they were much in demand. Their appearances brought high fees.

In early 1966 the Supremes had another hit, "The World Is Empty Without You." What made the Supremes special? What was this successful Supremes sound? Was it rock and roll? Diana Ross said the group's sound was not "deep rock 'n' roll." She explained, "It's more pleasant, more rounded and mellow. It's not shrill." Mary Wilson added, "It has the beat but not the grinding noise." The Supremes' sound took the country by storm.

The unbelievable success went on. In 1967 the Supremes earned seven Gold Records. All performers hope for at least one. The Supremes kept earning Gold Records with ease.

They didn't stand still. They didn't stick to one style only. They reworked standard songs by Rodgers and Hart, who had written several famous musicals, like *Oklahoma!*

They gave the old standbys a wholly new sound. They experimented with country westerns. They tried to reach out in new directions.

The Supremes had many successful singles. Soon they began to have success with albums like "Meet the Supremes" and "Country Western and Pop."

At this time the Supremes hired a new writing team. The team of Holland, Dozier, and Holland had brought them fame and success. But the music had a certain sound. The Supremes wanted something different. In 1968 the new team created another highly successful song.

There were other changes. Cindy Birdsong replaced Florence Ballard. Diana Ross was, of course, the most famous member. The name of the group was changed to "Diana Ross and the Supremes." As always, the trio went on tours, by this time with a Motown orchestra.

Nothing stands still. Change is always with us. In 1970 Diana Ross left the group and began to perform alone. Just before Diana left the group, the singers made a last hit record together. It was called "Someday We'll Be Together." Jean Terrell replaced Diana in the group.

In her career alone, Diana continued the tradition of success. She played the best entertainment spots and earned very high fees. She sang Motown songs, but she tried other types of songs as well. Her appearance was as striking as her songs.

Her singing continued to win admiration even from hardboiled critics. A writer for *Time* said her voice was as smooth and soft as velvet.

In April 1971 Diana had a television special called simply *Diana*. Bill Cosby and the Jackson Five joined the performance. Diana did more than sing. She gave excellent impressions of Harpo Marx, W. C. Fields, and Charlie Chaplin. She demonstrated that she was a woman with many talents, not just one.

Another talent was soon to be shown. In 1972 she played the part of Billie Holiday in *Lady Sings the Blues.* Her acting was singled out for approval. William Wolf of *Cue* magazine wrote, "If there's any justice, Diana Ross should be the biggest movie superstar to come along since Barbra Streisand, and she possesses deeper acting ability."

Diana was named *Female Entertainer of the Year* in 1970 and received a Grammy Award as leading female vocalist. She has continued to win awards for her many achievements. Her records still do well on the charts. "Upside Down" was number one in September 1980. "Endless Love," with Lionel Richie, made the top of the charts in August 1981.

Diana Ross's continuing popularity was again demonstrated in September 1984. She was scheduled for four concerts at the Radio City Music Hall in New York City. When her fans heard of this assignment, they gobbled up the tickets. Soon no tickets were left. Many fans were disappointed. To satisfy the demand, the sponsors added two more shows. To make room for the two extra concerts, the Radio City officials had to make some changes involving another entertainer. Peter Allen had been scheduled to give concerts in Radio City for those two extra days. Instead, his performances were moved to Carnegie Hall, also in New York City.

Diana has worked for good causes. Coretta Scott King and Reverend Ralph Abernathy have *commended* her publicly for her assistance to the Southern Christian Leadership Conference.

Diana Ross has traveled a long way from her home in a third-floor walk-up apartment in Detroit. But she has never forgotten her roots. She bought a new home for her mother and family. She continues to be close to those who loved her and encouraged her to become great.

UNDERSTANDING WHAT YOU HAVE READ

Finding Another Title

1. Another good title for this selection might be (a) The Gold Records of Diana Ross (b) The Making of Motown Records (c) The Courage and Talent of Diana Ross (d) A Star Is Born . . . Overnight.

Getting the Main Idea

2. Diana Ross (a) gave excellent impressions of other stars (b) has forgotten her roots in Detroit (c) gave credit for her success to her writers (d) has been a consistently successful performer.

Finding Details

3. The minister in Diana's family was her (a) grandfather (b) father (c) brother (d) husband.
4. The Primettes (a) were rivals of Diana Ross (b) later became the Supremes (c) were led by Lionel Richie (d) were also called the Shirelles.
5. Diana was disappointed when she tried out for a (a) Broadway play (b) television series (c) Hollywood movie (d) high school musical.
6. The Motown Record Corporation was formed by (a) Eddie Holland (b) Berry Gordy, Jr. (c) Lamont Dozier (d) Peter Allen.
7. Mary Wells is the name of (a) a singer (b) a talent scout (c) an owner of Motown (d) a writer.
8. Florence Ballard was replaced in the group by (a) Jean Terrell (b) Mary Wilson (c) Cindy Birdsong (d) Billie Holiday.

9. Diana Ross left the Supremes in (a) 1967 (b) 1968 (c) 1969 (d) 1970.
10. Diana did good impressions of all the following EXCEPT (a) Charlie Chaplin (b) W. C. Fields (c) Cary Grant (d) Harpo Marx.

Making Inferences

11. A quality that Diana showed even in high school was (a) ambition (b) nervousness (c) hopelessness (d) unfriendliness.
12. The first singing experiences of the Supremes could be called (a) remarkable (b) widely noticed (c) disappointing (d) cruel.
13. The Supremes were successful because they (a) played hard rock (b) made their name first in country music (c) developed their own kind of rock (d) left Motown after the first year.
14. When Diana recalls her childhood, she probably thinks that she was (a) remarkable (b) lucky (c) overworked (d) unfortunate.
15. Diana Ross believes that a performer should (a) not get into a rut (b) always stick with her original group (c) not give large concerts after turning 40 (d) avoid Hollywood and concentrate on television.

Predicting What Happens Next

16. When Diana Ross left the Supremes, she probably (a) did not approve of her replacement (b) refused to sing for Motown again (c) hoped the Supremes would fail (d) wished the new group good luck.

Deciding on the Order of Events

17. The following events are scrambled. Arrange them in proper order, as they happened. Use letters only.
    (a) Diana gives six concerts in Radio City Music Hall.
    (b) Diana sings in the church choir.
    (c) The Supremes sing for Motown Records.
    (d) Diana and her friends form the Primettes.

Inferring Tone

18. Geoffrey Cannon's attitude toward Berry Gordy, Jr. (283) is one of (a) disapproval (b) boredom (c) admiration (d) disrespect.

Separating Facts from Opinions

For each of the following, tell whether the statement is a fact (*F*) or an opinion (*O*).

19. Diana Ross should not have left the Supremes and gone on her own.

20. Diana Ross is the best popular singer of our time.

Understanding Words from Context

21. Diana lived in a low-income housing project in Detroit, but she never thought of her neighborhood as a *ghetto* when she was there.
    A *ghetto* (281) is a (a) poor, separate part of a city (b) business district in a city (c) small village on the outskirts of a city (d) theater district.

22. The three often *harmonized* on street corners and sang at parties.

Harmonized (282) means (a) dressed (b) sang together (c) played the harmonica (d) danced.

23. Gordy wanted black performers to be accepted worldwide. He "poured all his energy and money into what has been his most dramatic social achievement: getting *universal* acceptance, by means of Diana Ross, of the idea that black is beautiful."
    Universal (283) means (a) part (b) immediate (c) unexpected (d) general.

24. Of the six singles they recorded, six became hits. They were the only singing group in history to earn six *consecutive* Gold Records.
    Consecutive (284) means (a) solid (b) valuable (c) one after the other (d) popular.

25. Diana Ross worked for good causes. Coretta Scott King and Reverend Ralph Abernathy have *commended* her publicly.
    Commended (286) means (a) mentioned her name (b) praised (c) scolded (d) discovered.

THINKING IT OVER

1. How did Diana Ross show that she could hold to her course?
2. What part did Berry Gordy, Jr., play in her success?
3. What qualities are needed for a long and successful career in popular music?
4. Have you seen Diana Ross perform? Tell about your experience.
5. How important are writers to the success of a singer?
6. Do you know another person who rose from a poor childhood to success? How did this happen?
7. How did Diana demonstrate that she has talents in addition to singing?

ANOTHER LOOK AT THE QUOTATION

*When I'm pushing myself, testing
myself, that's when I'm happiest. That's
when the rewards are greatest.*
SISSY SPACEK

1. Explain the quotation in your own words.
2. How did Diana Ross show that she agreed with the quotation?
3. Do you work best under pressure? Explain.

WORDS AT YOUR SERVICE—SIMILES

A writer for *Time* said her voice was *as smooth and soft as velvet.* (285)
Diana's voice isn't actually velvet. It is as smooth and soft as velvet. Even though velvet and Diana's voice are quite different, the writer finds a basis for comparison. A comparison of unlike objects is called a *simile.*

Similes and metaphors both compare unlike objects.
Simile: Her voice is as smooth and soft as velvet.
Metaphor: She has a velvet voice.
A simile uses *as* (or *like*) to make the comparison. A metaphor makes the comparison without *like* or *as.*

Try your skill at completing similes. Match the items in column A with the items in column B.

A	B
1. as weary as	a. a constantly repeated commercial
2. as unspoiled as	
3. as boring as	b. sardines in a can
4. as nervous as	c. newly fallen snow
5. as crowded as	d. a cook after dinner
	e. a person at a job interview

Now try your skill at creating similes of your own. Complete each of the similes. Try to make your similes as effective as possible.

EXAMPLE
as bad-tempered as . . .
What might be bad-tempered? A hungry bear? A person with too little sleep? A wasp from a disturbed nest? Choose the simile you like best.

1. as lively as . . .
2. as bright as . . .
3. as colorful as . . .
4. as sweet as . . .
5. as confusing as . . .

COMPLETING AN OUTLINE

The article on Diana Ross might be outlined in the following way. Five outline items have been omitted. Test your understanding of the structure of the article by following the directions after the outline.

   I. The difficult field of popular music
      A.
      B. The exception: Diana Ross

  II. Diana Ross's early years
      A. Birth in Detroit
      B.
      C. Achievements in high school
      D. Formation of the Primettes
      E. First disappointment

III. The Motown Record Corporation
   A.
   B. Opportunities for black singers
   C. Diana's efforts to get a chance
   D. Renaming the Primettes

IV. The Supremes
   A.
   B. The smash hits
   C. The Supremes' sound
   D. Experimenting with new ideas
   E. Another set of writers

V. Diana on her own
   A. Success in personal appearances
   B.
   C. *Lady Sings the Blues*
   D. Many awards
   E. Continuing success

Fill in the items omitted from the outline. Correctly match the items in column A with the outline numbers in column B, which show where each item belongs in the outline.

A	B
1. The new writers	a. I. A.
2. Singing in church choir	b. II. B.
	c. III. A.
3. TV special—*Diana*	d. IV. A.
4. Berry Gordy, Jr.,'s contribution	e. V. B.
5. Ups and downs of performers	

5

ANOTHER LOOK

HOW MUCH DO YOU REMEMBER?

1. The youngest person to win success is **(a)** Mary Lou Retton **(b)** Tom Selleck **(c)** Beverly Sills **(d)** Diana Ross.

2. The two most closely associated with music are **(a)** Mary Lou Retton and Diana Ross **(b)** Tom Selleck and Beverly Sills **(c)** Beverly Sills and Diana Ross **(d)** Mary Lou Retton and Tom Selleck.

3. The person who at first won more fame in Europe than in the United States is **(a)** Mary Lou Retton **(b)** Tom Selleck **(c)** Diana Ross **(d)** Beverly Sills.

4. Ecaterina Szabo is **(a)** an opera singer **(b)** a Rumanian gymnast **(c)** a star on *Magnum, P.I.* **(d)** a pop singer.

5. Which of the following is NOT correctly matched?
   (a) Mary Lou Retton—Olympics winner
   (b) Tom Selleck—professional baseball player
   (c) Beverly Sills—opera star
   (d) Diana Ross—actress and singer

6. The American women's gymnastic teams (a) had only one medal in the years before 1984 (b) had twice beaten teams from the Soviet Union in the years before 1984 (c) had several members from Mary Lou Retton's family (d) did not take part in the 1984 Olympics.

7. The person who became director of the New York City Opera is (a) Berry Gordy, Jr. (b) Roger Ebert (c) Julianne McNamara (d) Beverly Sills.

8. The person who was given a start by Berry Gordy, Jr., is (a) Beverly Sills (b) Tom Selleck (c) Diana Ross (d) Mary Lou Retton.

9. *Motown* was named after (a) New York City (b) Chicago (c) Detroit (d) Los Angeles.

10. All the subjects in this unit (a) kept working hard and trying (b) won success more through luck than effort (c) became famous in the movies (d) had unhappy childhoods.

WHAT IS YOUR OPINION?

1. Success sometimes comes quickly and easily. Usually, though, it is the result of hard work. How did the subjects in this unit win success? Give examples to prove your point.

2. Mary Lou Retton and Diana Ross are in entirely different fields. Yet they are alike in some ways. Explain.

3. How did Beverly Sills help the cause of women's rights?

4. Do you like Tom Selleck on television? What qualities do you most admire?

5. *Magnum, P.I.* is a kind of private-eye show. Do you enjoy these programs on television? Do you like other types of shows better? Explain, with examples.

THE QUOTATION AND THE UNIT

Success is a journey, not a destination.
BEN SWEETLAND

1. Explain the quotation in your own words.
2. Why is the quotation suitable for a unit on "Holding to the Course"?
3. What is success? Is it fame? plenty of money? good family ties? Give your idea of true success.
4. How did Beverly Sills prove that success is a journey, not a destination?
5. Do we appreciate success more if it doesn't come too easily? Explain.